DRS. SAMPSON DAVIS, GEORGE JENKINS, RAMECK HUNT
AND *THE PACT*

"Sampson Davis, Rameck Hunt, and George Jenkins—M.D., M.D., and D.M.D., respectively—are something more than the sum of their degrees."                                    —*Newsday*

"[A] prescription for success."          —*The Philadelphia Inquirer*

"Eye-opening and moving. . . *The Pact* is a lesson in the power of peers."                          —*The Atlanta Journal-Constitution*

"A powerful message of hope to inner-city youngsters."
                                    —*The Dallas Morning News*

"While their story is sometimes tragic, sometimes funny and sometimes remarkable, it is always inspirational."
                                    —*St. Louis Post-Dispatch*

"Will inspire and entertain . . . *The Pact* is the impressive true story of three teenage boys from Newark, New Jersey, who became outstanding men."                          —*Essence*

"Starkly honest . . . a dramatic firsthand narrative detailing how each doctor managed to rise above the ills of city life—violence, drugs and poverty—to achieve what once seemed like a far-fetched dream."
                                    —*The Newark Star-Ledger*

"It is probably the most important book for African-American families that has been written since the protest era. . . . Get *The Pact*. It just may change a teen's future."          —*Chicago Sun-Times*

## ABOUT THE AUTHORS

George Jenkins, Rameck Hunt, and Sampson Davis grew up together in Newark, New Jersey, and graduated from Seton Hall University. Davis and Hunt received their medical degrees from the Robert Wood Johnson Medical School, and Jenkins his dentistry degree from the University of Medicine and Dentistry of New Jersey. All three are recipients of the *Essence* Lifetime Achievement Award. Together they created the Three Doctors Foundation, which offers a yearly scholarship to a promising Newark student entering a four-year college.

Lisa Frazier Page is a winner of the National Association of Black Journalists Award for features. She has been a writer for *The Washington Post* since 1995, and was an award-winning reporter and columnist for New Orleans's *Times-Picayune* for nearly a decade. Page, who is married and the mother of three children, lives in the Washington, D.C., area.

## TELL US YOUR STORY

The Three Doctors are **looking for incredible stories of triumph**. If you or someone you know traveled through extraordinary paths by overcoming and persevering in order to survive and accomplish goals, please write us at:

**The Three Doctors**
**65 Hazelwood Ave.**
**Newark, NJ 07106**

or email **www.threedoctors.com** and share your story.

# The Pact

*Three Young Men Make a Promise*

*and Fulfill a Dream*

DRS. SAMPSON DAVIS, GEORGE JENKINS,

AND RAMECK HUNT

*with Lisa Frazier Page*

RIVERHEAD BOOKS

New York

Riverhead Books
Published by The Berkley Publishing Group
A division of Penguin Group (USA) Inc.
375 Hudson Street
New York, New York 10014

While the authors have made every effort to provide accurate
telephone numbers and Internet addresses at the time of publication,
neither the publisher nor the authors assume any responsibility for errors,
or for changes that occur after publication.

First Riverhead hardcover edition: May 2002
First Riverhead trade paperback edition: May 2003
Riverhead trade paperback ISBN: 1-57322-989-X

The Library of Congress has catalogued the Riverhead hardcover edition as follows:

Davis, Sampson.
The pact / by Sampson Davis, George Jenkins, and Rameck Hunt.
p.   cm.
ISBN 1-57322-216-X
1. African American physicians—Biography.   I. Jenkins, George.
II. Hunt, Rameck.   III. Title.
R695.D38     2002
610'.92'2—dc21                     2001059647

Printed in the United States of America

20 19 18 17 16 15

# CONTENTS

# INTRODUCTION

WE TREAT THEM in our hospitals every day.

They are young brothers, often drug dealers, gang members, or small-time criminals, who show up shot, stabbed, or beaten after a hustle gone bad. To some of our medical colleagues, they are just nameless thugs, perpetuating crime and death in neighborhoods that have seen far too much of those things. But when we look into their faces, we see ourselves as teenagers, we see our friends, we see what we easily could have become as young adults. And we're reminded of the thin line that separates us—three twenty-nine-year-old doctors (an emergency-room physician, an internist, and a dentist)—from these patients whose lives are filled with danger and desperation.

We grew up in poor, broken homes in New Jersey neighborhoods riddled with crime, drugs, and death, and came of age in the 1980s at the height of a crack epidemic that ravaged communities like ours throughout the nation. There were no doctors or lawyers walking the streets of our communities. Where we lived, hustlers reigned, and it was easy to follow their example. Two of us landed in juvenile-detention centers before our eighteenth birthdays. But inspired early by caring and imaginative role models, one of us in childhood latched on to a dream of becoming a dentist, steered clear of trouble, and in his senior year of high school persuaded his two best friends to apply to a college program for minority students interested in becoming doctors. We knew we'd never survive if we went after it alone. And so we made a pact: we'd help one another through, no matter what.

In college, the three of us stuck together to survive and thrive in a world that was different from anything we had ever known. We provided one another with a kind of positive peer pressure. From the moment we made our pact, the competition was on. When one of us finished his college application, the other two rushed to send theirs out. When we participated in a six-week remedial program at Seton Hall University the summer before our freshman year, each of us felt pressured to perform well because we knew our friends would excel and we didn't want to embarrass ourselves or lag behind. When one of us made an A on a test, the others strived to make A's, too.

We studied together. We worked summer jobs together. We partied together. And we learned to solve our problems together. We are doctors today because of the positive influences that we had on one another.

The lives of most impressionable young people are

defined by their friends, whether they are black, white, Hispanic, or Asian; whether they are rich, poor, or middle-class; whether they live in the city, the suburbs, or the country. Among boys, particularly, there seems to be some macho code that says to gain respect, you have to prove that you're bad. We know firsthand that the wrong friends can lead you to trouble. But even more, they can tear down hopes, dreams, and possibilities. We know, too, that the right friends inspire you, pull you through, rise with you.

Each of us experienced friendships that could have destroyed our lives. We suspect that many of the young brothers we treat every day in our hospitals are entangled in such friendships—friendships that require them to prove their toughness and manhood daily, even at the risk of losing their own lives. The three of us were blessed. We found in one another a friendship that works in a powerful way; a friendship that helped three vulnerable boys grow into successful men; a friendship that ultimately helped save our lives.

But it wasn't always easy. There were times when one of us was ready to give up, and times when we made bad decisions. Some of that is ugly and difficult to admit, and we suffered pain and other consequences. But we have laid it all out here nonetheless.

We did this because we hope that our story will inspire others, so that even those young people who feel trapped by their circumstances, or pulled by peer pressure in the wrong directions, might look for a way out not through drugs, alcohol, crime, or dares but through the power of friendship. And within our story are many others, of mentors, friends, relatives, and even strangers we met along the way, whose good-will and good deeds made a difference in our lives. We hope our story will also demonstrate that anyone with enough compassion has the power to transform and redirect someone else's troubled life.

If we have succeeded at all in helping to turn even a single life around or in opening a window of hope, then this book was well worth our effort.

# 1

## DREAMING BIG

### *George*

MY EYES FOLLOWED the dentist's gloved hands from the silver tray next to my chair to my wide-open mouth.

"What's that for?" I asked, pointing at the funny-looking pliers he was holding.

At eleven, I sported a set of seriously crooked teeth, and my mother had taken me to the University of Medicine and Dentistry in Newark to get braces that we hoped would improve my smile.

My curiosity must have impressed the dentist, because he not only explained his tools and how he planned to use them; he also taught me the names and number of teeth and how to count and classify them. A few minutes later, he quizzed me to see how much I remembered.

Our little game left me so excited that I could hardly wait for my next appointment. That was when I began thinking about becoming a dentist someday.

I don't remember the dentist's name, but I never forgot what he did for me. He gave me a dream. And there was no greater gift for a smart kid growing up in a place where dreams were snatched away all the time.

I spent the first seven years of my life in Apartment 5G of the Stella Wright Housing Projects with my mother and older brother. Our building was a graffiti-covered, thirteen-story high-rise with elevators that smelled like urine and sometimes didn't work. Like public-housing projects in major cities across the country, the Stella Wright development was massive: sixteen high-rises stretched over two blocks. They were packed with hundreds of poor families like mine, mostly mothers and children, few fathers in sight.

My favorite place was the playground. But like so many structures around the development, it stayed in disrepair. My friends and I were constantly climbing, jumping, and swinging on broken-down equipment that daily threatened our lives.

One day when I was five, I was playing on the wooden jungle gym and tried to skip over a missing plank to get to the sliding board. My jump was short, and I missed. My small body slipped through the gap and slammed to the ground below. The impact knocked me unconscious.

My brother, Garland, just six and a half then, rushed over, slapped my face over and over again, and tried to scoop my body up in his arms, thinking I was dead. Blood gushed from the back of my head. He screamed for our mother.

Our mother, Ella Jenkins Mack, has always been the dominant figure in my life. I was just a toddler when she and my father, George Jenkins, Sr., divorced. When I was two, we moved from South Carolina, where I was born, to Newark. I rarely saw my father after that. He came around a few times while I was in high school, sent $500 or so for toys at Christmas, and attended my graduations. But we never spent the kind of time together that builds a relationship.

As soon as my mother, my brother, and I moved to the projects in a building on Muhammad Ali Avenue, my mom started working to get us out. She was a proud woman, and she didn't like living in public housing. She wanted to make it on her own. Raised on a farm with eight brothers and sisters in Warrenton, South Carolina, she had been taught to fend for herself. She developed a toughness that at times made her seem emotionless, but her determination and consistency stabilized our lives. I never saw life break her down. If she struggled to pay the bills—and I know there must have been times when she did—her children never saw it. When Garland and I did well, she praised us without gushing. And we knew better than to expect a reward for doing what we were expected to do, like cleaning our room or making a good grade on a report card.

Mom began working as a financial customer-service representative for Chubb Insurance Company in 1978 and still works there today. By the time I was seven, she had saved enough to move us out of the projects. We moved a block away to High Park Gardens, a private complex with landscaped gardens, grass, and a few trees. The complex operated like a co-op. Each tenant bought stock for $2,400 and got a discount on the rent. We could see our old building in the projects from the back window.

Four years later, my mother married Garland's father, Heyward Mack, a decent and quiet man with a Southern drawl that tied him to his South Carolina roots. He had been around for most of my life, but we never connected emotionally. He didn't treat me differently because I was his stepson. It just seemed he was at a loss for how to develop a relationship with me, or even with his biological son when he reentered our lives full-time. My stepfather didn't care much for sports, so we couldn't bond while watching the Knicks on television or sharing hot dogs at Mets games at Shea Stadium. He always seemed to be working on cars, but he never pulled us under the hood with him for the kind of interaction that can bring a father and son together. He kept mostly to himself and played an auxiliary role, more like an uncle, transporting us where we needed to go and occasionally giving us money. He wasn't unkind, and I know at times he must have felt like an outsider who could never quite break into the tight triangle that was my mother, my brother, and I.

Six years into the marriage, Garland and I returned to the apartment after school one day and noticed that the VCR was missing from its spot underneath the television in the living room. We walked from room to room and discovered that in our parents' bedroom someone had rifled the dresser drawers and left them open. We were sure we had been robbed. I called Mom as quickly as my fingers could press the numbers. When I told her what had happened, she started laughing. It seemed a strange response for a woman who had just learned she had been ripped off. But she knew the truth: my stepfather had packed all of his stuff and left.

Just like that, he was gone.

The closest thing to a father I ever knew was my friend's dad, Shahid Jackson. Shahid, Jr., was one of the first kids I met in the new apartment complex. Everybody called him Cash. He attended Spencer Elementary, too, and we hit it off right away. He was a quiet, passive guy, and I was the big-brother type, so our personalities complemented each other. We never argued. We played video games at his house every day. His father was the coolest dad I had ever met. He treated me like I was one of his sons. He was the kind of dad who often bent the rules in the child's favor.

With his boisterous personality, Mr. Jackson was as comfortable talking to a crack dealer on the corner as he was chatting with the mayor. As a bodyguard to stars, including Smokey Robinson and Muhammad Ali, he traveled frequently when we were in elementary school. When he returned from his road trips, he showered us all with gifts. Whatever he bought for his two sons, he bought for me, too.

When he eventually joined the police force and took over the Police Athletic League, we played on his baseball and basketball teams. He took us fishing and to work out with him in the gym. We often just rode around town in his van and stopped to eat at restaurants. He was the first person to take me out for Portuguese food and the first to introduce me to filet mignon, which he cooked himself. One of his favorite stops was a deli called Cooper's, where we ordered the best triple-decker sandwiches I've ever eaten.

Mr. Jackson always let me know he believed in me. When I told him while I was in high school that I'd enrolled in the Pre-

Medical/Pre-Dental Plus Program at Seton Hall with two of
my friends, he wasn't surprised. From that point on, when he
talked about my future, he always prefaced his remarks with
"When you become a doctor . . ."

I was still barely able to imagine that myself.

In many ways, Mom was my father, too. She was, until she
married my stepfather, the family's sole provider. We were
lucky to have a babysitter who treated us like her own children—Miss Willie, an old-fashioned woman who lived three
blocks away. Sometimes, when she was working full-time,
Mom dropped us off before sunrise and couldn't pick us up
until nightfall because she had to work late. If either of us was
sick or if it was too cold or stormy outside, Miss Willie
insisted that Garland and I stay overnight at her house so
Mom wouldn't have to drive us back and forth in the bad
weather. She even took care of us for several days when my
mother went into the hospital.

But when I turned six, Mom gave us keys to the apartment, and we started going home alone after school. We had
to call her at work as soon as we made it indoors.

Because of her steady job, our pantry and refrigerator
were always full of food. We didn't move around constantly
like some families did but lived in the same apartment for the
rest of my childhood. And Mom kept the utility bills paid, too.
I was fortunate; most of the guys I know who got into trouble
in my neighborhood had circumstances at home that weren't
as stable. Many guys I knew sold drugs because they felt they
had no choice. And I believe that kids who grew up in less stable environments were more susceptible to pressure from

friends to do the negative things that everyone else seemed to be doing.

Sam and Rameck faced those pressures all the time.

I wasn't any smarter or more special than the guys around me. For some reason, throughout my life I was blessed with people who told me positive things, and I believed them. I believed my third-grade teacher when she told me that I could go to college and have a great career someday if I just stayed out of trouble. So I hung out with kids who were like me, trying to do the right thing. Most of the time they were either my age or a bit younger. The older guys seemed too advanced, too ready to rush into the life I was trying to avoid.

Even when, as a teenager, I tried to hang out with Garland and his friends, he wouldn't allow it. He wasn't necessarily trying to protect me. He just didn't want his kid brother hanging around. But it kept me away from a group of guys who weren't the least bit interested in school. I always wished for a little brother or sister, so I became a big brother to my friends.

Sure, I wanted other kids to think I was cool. What kid doesn't? But I'd decided then that I wasn't going to do certain things, like sell drugs, and I just stuck to my decision.

Guys in the neighborhood, even the gun-toting tough guys who stayed in trouble, didn't hassle me about doing well in school. If they laughed at me or called me punk, geek, nerd, or corny, they did so behind my back. I walked the same dangerous streets as the guys selling drugs and stealing cars, and I was cool with many of them. I didn't look down on them, and they didn't bother me. It was as if there was some silent acknowledgment between us that they were doing what they believed they had to do, and so was I.

As soon as I was responsible enough to work, I got a job. I was thirteen when Blonnie Watson, president of the board that operates High Park Gardens, hired me as a groundskeeper at the complex. She liked me and went out of her way to be kind and encouraging. I earned minimum wage picking up trash around the building and doing minor chores, but I was thrilled to be able to afford some of the trendy clothes and shoes that my mother refused to buy.

Because Mom worked so much, she had little time to visit the schools my brother and I attended or talk to our teachers. She went to open-house meetings every now and then and fussed if we brought home bad grades on our report cards. But she was not a check-your-homework-every-night kind of mom. She was too exhausted when she got home from work. My brother took full advantage of her leniency. He chose to tolerate the verbal punishment at report-card time rather than buckle down, study, and bring home decent grades.

I loved school. My third-grade teacher, Viola Johnson, was largely responsible for that. By then we were out of the projects, but like most of the kids in my class, I was poor. That meant nothing to me then because I never felt deprived, especially in Miss Johnson's class. She was a tiny ball of energy with a high-pitched girlish voice and the same honey-colored complexion as my mother.

Miss Johnson had lived in Newark since she was four years old. She attended public schools and followed her father's trail into teaching. Once she began teaching, she was always taking classes somewhere—a drama class here, a literature class there. And she brought what she learned to her classroom.

When I met her, Ms. Johnson was in her mid-forties, single with no children. I guess her students filled that space in her heart, because she nurtured us like a mother. She told us that college was not just an option, but the next step to advancement, like the thirteenth grade.

"Everybody has a chance to go to college," she said. "Never say you can't go because of money. Get that degree. You must get that degree."

She regularly got discount tickets for us to attend Broadway plays. She asked parents to pay for the tickets, and we rode to New York City on a bus that she usually rented herself. And we did not dare dress tacky. Miss Johnson required the girls to wear dresses and stockings and the guys to wear nice slacks and shirts.

She also secured the scripts of popular plays, assigned roles, and rehearsed us so that we could perform for the entire school. When we put on a production of *Annie*, I played Daddy Warbucks.

Miss Johnson introduced us to algebra and Shakespeare with books written for kids. We even formed a Shakespeare club that met on Tuesdays after school. I was elected president. We read and discussed Shakespeare at our meetings. At one meeting, the club voted on our official uniform: burgundy sweaters with the group's name, "The Shakespeare Club," embroidered over the pocket. Once, we wore our sweaters to a concert at Symphony Hall. Several people in the audience asked Miss Johnson which private school we attended. She smiled, held her head high, and announced with great pride that we were from Louise A. Spencer Elementary, a public school in the Central Ward, which practically everyone in Newark considered the ghetto.

Our teacher loved to travel, and she always sent us postcards and bought us souvenirs from wherever she went. Some days, she pulled the globe from the corner of the classroom, gathered us around her, and told us stories about places that before were just spots on a map to us.

Noise didn't seem to bother Miss Johnson, as long as children were engaged in learning. She stayed with us after school to dye eggs for Easter, make gingerbread men for Christmas, or bake cookies, just because.

Miss Johnson retired from Newark's public schools in 1993 after thirty-two years of teaching and moved to Johnsonville, West Virginia, a tiny town named after her great-grandfather. I lost touch with her when I left Spencer and for years didn't know where she had gone.

But I never forgot her. She made a lanky, mild-mannered kid growing up in a tough place feel smart and special. She also made me curious about the world I had yet to see. That was the curiosity the dentist saw in me the day I showed up at his office to get braces.

# 2

## HOME

### *Sam*

I WAS EIGHT YEARS OLD, walking one afternoon with Moms toward Broad and Market streets in downtown Newark, where we'd come to do some shopping. In those days, Woolworth's, McCrory's, and other discount and department stores, and low-budget restaurants and movie theaters, brought people in from all over the city. The streets were bustling, and I held Moms's hand and gazed up at the store signs and placards in the windows, putting letters together to figure out words.

My eyes were fixed on a sign outside a store.

"What's that word?" I asked.

My mother was silent for a moment.

"I don't know, Marshall," she said softly, calling me, as usual, by my middle name.

She tugged my hand to go. I planted my feet to stay.

"I gotta know!" I screamed. "I gotta know!"

Moms often tells that story when people ask her what I was like as a child. I don't remember it, but I do remember always asking questions. My eyes took in everything, and back then, Moms was the first person I turned to for an interpretation. It was not the first or last time she would not be able to provide an answer. Though she tried hard to hide it for much of my childhood, I soon figured out her secret. My mother, Ruthener Davis, had never learned to read.

She was born in 1933, the fourth child of a rural South Carolina farmer and a housewife. She was just seven when her mother died, leaving her in the care of a grandmother for the next five years. Moms has always been a nurturer, so when she returned home to live with her father, two older brothers, and a sister, she dropped out of school to wash, cook, clean, and care for her family. Back then, education seemed a luxury to her. She wanted to go to school, but her obligation to family was more important. At fifteen, she married my father, Kenneth Davis, after spotting him, dressed in his Army uniform, at a local carnival. He was a handsome man with medium-brown skin and a slender build. She's always been petite, only five feet tall.

Pop was discharged honorably from the Army, and he and Moms lived with his relatives in South Carolina for their first ten years together. My three older siblings—Kenneth, Jr., Roselene, and Fellease—were born there. Around 1958, Pop took the advice of an aunt who lived in New York and migrated north with his family in search of a better-paying job. They landed in Newark.

Pop found a job fueling airplanes at the Newark airport with a company called Butler Aviation, where he would work for the next thirty-five years. Pop loved his job and periodically took his three youngest children—Andre, Carlton, and me—to the airport to see the planes. We would sit in the cockpit and pretend we were flying them. Moms was pregnant with my brother Andre in 1968, when Pop suggested they use his GI Bill to buy a house. Their search ended at a modest two-bedroom wood-frame house with a finished basement on Ludlow Street. It was a poor working-class community with a mixture of black and Latino families in an area known for a notorious public-housing development called the Dayton Street projects. A row of small single-family houses sat on one side of the street; a graveyard and the sprawling high-rise projects, officially named the Rev. Otto E. Kretchmer Homes, sat on the other.

Even then, the projects had a reputation for regular stabbings, muggings, and shootings, but the 1980s, the decade when I came of age, would usher in a level of crime and violence that would make it hard for me to imagine surviving to the age of twenty-five.

I was born at Beth Israel Hospital in Newark on January 19, 1973, and brought home to Ludlow Street. One of my earliest memories is heading to preschool with my shoulder-length, curly black hair parted in the middle and braided into long plaits. Moms refused to cut it, despite the suggestion from school administrators who told her that some teachers and students were mistaking me for a girl. Finally, Moms relented and took me to the barber. When he snipped off my plaits, she got down on her hands and knees and began stuffing my hair into a plastic bag. Once we made it home, she pulled out the family Bible and placed my hair inside.

"I'm keeping you in here," she said.

Moms relied on a power greater than herself to raise black boys in an era when the streets were claiming too many. I've often thought about my hair in that Bible, especially when I found myself in tight situations with seemingly no way out, and then, unexpectedly, a door opened.

Three years after I was born, my brother Carlton came along. Moms describes those years as the happiest of her life. It was as close as she would ever get to the picket-fence life she had always imagined. Neighbors and parishioners from St. Thomas Aquinas Roman Catholic Church, which sits in the middle of the block on the single-family side of Ludlow, came bearing food and gifts after the birth. When Pop cashed his paycheck, he placed the crisp bills in a legal-sized envelope and brought it home to Moms. She could stretch a dollar farther than anyone I had ever seen, and her sole job was to take care of the family.

Moms was known as the mother of the entire neighborhood. She rose every morning about four A.M. and picked up the empty soda and beer cans, potato-chip bags, candy wrappers, and other trash left along the walkway the night before. Then she swept the street, working her way up to the church. She did this faithfully every day. I wasn't mature enough then to understand that this was her contribution to her church and community. She had little else to give. Instead, I felt embarrassed. And I took some serious ribbing from friends who found it funny that my mother was up at four in the morning sweeping the streets.

My pop loved music, especially jazz, blues, and gospel quartets. On some holidays and weekends, he dragged his guitar and amplifier into the living room, put on a Dixie Hummingbirds, Ray Charles, Mills Brothers, or Count Basie album, turned the volume on the record player as loud as it would go, and strummed along. The music filled the entire house and drifted outside, far down the street. I would sit in the doorway between the living room and kitchen or on the stairs with one of my brothers, playing with our plastic green Army men, watching our father, who seemed oblivious to our presence. The music took him someplace else. We usually got restless and scurried off to play, leaving him still strumming in the living room.

I couldn't stand that old music. Life is funny, though. Those days in the living room with Pop, his guitar, and his music were among the times I missed most when he left.

Like most kids, I wanted my family to be like the ones I saw on television, the Cleavers, the Bradys, the Huxtables. But I never saw those parents argue and fight the way mine did. I suppose the constant pressure of trying to raise six children on blue-collar wages in a world often hostile to black families, especially black men, created an environment full of tension. Our house at times felt like a gunpowder keg, and on Saturday nights, the least little spark would cause it to blow.

"Your daddy ain't shit," Moms would yell to us after one of her heated exchanges with our father.

Just as often, those words came from Pop: "Your mama ain't shit."

He sometimes hit her. She slashed his tires. He drew his gun. Those were terrifying moments for my younger brother and me. We listened from another room as our parents' angry voices and the sounds of blows came crashing through the walls. When they fought in front of us, my brother and I clung helplessly to each other until one of our parents walked away.

But even with all the fighting, it never occurred to me that one of them would actually leave us. Things always seemed to blow over pretty quickly, and life became normal again, Pop going off to work and bringing his entire paycheck home, and Moms cleaning, cooking, and washing all day. We didn't own a washing machine for a long time, so she scrubbed our clothes by hand on an old washboard she'd brought from South Carolina, then hung them out to dry on the clothesline in the backyard.

Then one day, Pop walked in and announced that he wanted a divorce. Moms suspected he'd met someone else. She pleaded and prayed he would come to his senses. But she had long ago learned that by the time Kenneth Davis, Sr., opened up to reveal his feelings, he had already worked out a resolution in his mind. Sure enough, a few days later, Moms responded to a knock at the front door and found a stranger standing there to serve her with papers.

I was eleven when the divorce became final. During the court hearing, which we all attended, Carlton, then just eight, cried all the way through. Pop had tried to reassure us that he would always be a part of our lives, but as a kid, you can't help feeling abandoned when a parent leaves so suddenly. I remember wondering: What are we going to do now? How are we going to make it?

It wouldn't be fair to say that Pop walked out completely. He did what he agreed to do and more. He paid the mortgage, which kept a roof over our heads. He came around to visit. We visited him. If one of us was sick, he rushed home or to the hospital to check on us. He sent what money he could for gifts during holidays. And for most major events in my life—baseball games, school programs, and graduations—he was there. I loved my father then, as I do now. But when he left, so did his regular paycheck and the security of knowing that all the bills would get paid and that my little brother and I would always have something to eat. My older brothers and sisters were in and out.

Moms had never worked, and with little education she had few marketable skills. We had to go on welfare. Moms was already leaning on me for things she couldn't do, like reading her mail, making deposits at the bank, and helping to write money orders for bills. It felt good to be responsible for such heavyweight duties at my age, but it was a burden that no eleven-year-old should have to bear. I felt responsible for helping her take care of the household. That might sound strange, since I was one of the younger ones and had four older brothers and sisters. But they were going through their own stages of rebellion and upheaval and were little help.

I couldn't do much but worry. There were days when we woke up with not enough food in the house to make a decent meal and no money to buy more.

"I'll make a way," Moms would say.

I've always admired her survivor instinct. Just as she'd promised, she came through, even if it meant calling to ask an out-of-town relative to wire some emergency cash or relying on neighbors or members of her church to bring us food. When the electric company turned off our power, we ran an extension cord from our house to the one next door until the bill could be paid. When the boiler went out in the dead of winter because we couldn't afford to buy more oil, we gathered around the stove in the kitchen, sometimes the only room in the house with heat. She chopped wood for the fireplace to help keep us warm in the winter. And she wore the same clothes year after year so that she could buy us sneakers and clothes for each new school year.

With the exception of Andre, my older brothers and sisters were all grown, in their twenties and thirties, when our parents broke up. But they never really left home for good. They would move out, live on their own for a few months or years, then move back, sometimes with their spouses and children. When it came to the family and our house, Moms had an open-door policy. She extended that policy to cousins and uncles, who also moved in with us at different times when they had no place to go. My cousin Thurmond, who lived with us off and on, was the kind of guy who lived for the moment. If he got paid on Friday, he was broke by Monday. When I got older and started working, he sometimes asked me if he could borrow $10 or $20 until his next check. He paid me back double. Sometimes I suspected that his true intention was to put a few extra dollars in my pockets. Our small house always seemed to be teeming with people. Once, I counted twelve, which included two older brothers and their wives and children, a cousin, Carlton, and me. And none of these occupants was financially stable enough to help buy food or pay the bills. Providing for so many must have put a lot of stress on my mother, but I don't ever recall her kicking her grown children or relatives out of the house because they didn't contribute.

My parents had two generations of children: Kenny, Roselene, and Fellease; then Andre, me, and Carlton. When Kenny was in his twenties and I was in preschool and elementary school, I worshipped him. He was a classy guy who always wore the latest fashions and listened to good '70s music—the Temptations, the Whispers, you name the black artists of the day and Kenny was in touch with their music. He went into the Army for a brief stint after high school and soon afterward had two sons, one my age and the other three years older. He married a woman named Ruthie and lived with her in the Seth Boyden Projects, a set of redbrick, low-rise apartments a few blocks from our house. Ruthie died suddenly in the late 1980s, and Kenny's life seemed to plunge into despair. He drank all the time and became belligerent and mean. When he showed up at our house, he ranted and raved, cursed, and threatened our mother. I went from worshipping him to hating him. I realize now that I just hated what had become of him.

I've never gotten to know the real Roselene. Moms likes to talk about how smart and productive her oldest daughter once was. She finished high school and in the early 1970s landed a job with the Mutual Benefit Company, which at the time was considered a major accomplishment for a black woman without a college degree. But that is not the Roselene I remember. I do recall trips with her to the movies and to her church. But the Roselene I remember most suffered from some kind of mental problem that made her paranoid and compulsive. She would wash her hands with Pine-Sol a hundred times a day. She wouldn't touch a doorknob if she had seen someone touch it before her, and she wouldn't sit on a toilet seat without scouring it if someone had sat on it since her last cleaning. She would walk around mumbling to herself, wearing the same clothes day after day. We tried many times to have her committed to the hospital for treatment of her mental condition, but she insisted she didn't have a problem, and the hospital sent her right back home. I never knew how to talk to her or how to reach her. With age, she seems to have improved somewhat, but her illness and the twenty-one-year age difference between us created a distance that, sadly, time has yet to close.

Of all my siblings, I was closest to Fellease, who later changed her name to Fenice. She is fourteen years older, but she always had time for me. She used to take me out for ice cream or to the movies. She was sassy and fun-loving, and she always knew the hottest song and the coolest new dance. On the street, she had a reputation as a sister not to mess with without some serious hell to pay. For me, Fel's little brother, her rep offered a measure of protection. Fellease dropped out of high school, married young, divorced, married again, and followed her new husband to his U.S. Army assignment in Hawaii, where she returned to school and earned a high-school-equivalency diploma. They split up a few years later, and she moved home. I was about fourteen when she returned. That's when we really grew close. We stayed up many nights until the early hours of morning, talking, playing spades, Pokeno, and Monopoly. She was a natural storyteller, and I loved listening to her talk about life in the family before I was born.

Fel always kept a job, so she would move out for a few months, then move back in when she fell on hard times. She was functional, but she was also a drug addict. I suspected it long before I knew for sure. Once, soon after she moved back home from Hawaii, she received a package from the islands in the mail. Moms assumed it was for her and tore into it. Inside was an Alka-Seltzer box packed with a pound of weed.

Another time, I was looking for something in the room where Fel slept and found a burnt spoon and a crack pipe. The pipe was a tiny nip bottle of Bacardi rum with a long, thin glass tube attached. I left it there and pushed what I had just confirmed to the back of mind with everything else I didn't want to face. I had a make-believe spot in the back of my mind—I thought of it as a trunk or Pandora's box—where I placed my bad experiences, stored them, and sealed them forever (or so I thought). When my parents argued, what I saw and heard went into that box. When my dad left, what I felt went into the box as well. I rarely cried. Later, I would meet someone who would help me open that box and for the first time deal with all that was in there. It would nearly scare me to death.

In the years to come, my sister's addiction and reckless

ways would get the best of her. And I would be saddled with the guilt of being unable to help.

Andre is the most stable of my older siblings. He reminds me of our mother. He's a hardworking man quick to open his door to a struggling family member or friend. He dropped out of high school in the tenth grade and married at the age of seventeen, but he went to work for the city of Newark as a groundskeeper in the beautiful Weequahic Park in 1987 and has been there ever since. He and his wife were already parents by the time they got married, but the marriage ended in a bitter divorce after just five years. Andre met someone else, had a second daughter, and has maintained a steady relationship with the child's mother for the past seven years.

Just four years older than I am, Andre was the brother I wanted to follow around the neighborhood. But who wants a little brother tagging along? He often pulled tricks to get rid of me. He'd say, "Marshall, go to the house and get your toys while we wait for you." When I came back, of course, he and his friends would be gone. He mostly hung out with his god-brothers, Orlando and Edwin, and other neighborhood friends, Frank, Billy, Willie, Modesto, and Leslie.

One day I managed to end up with them at a small grass park that had several benches, basically green wooden slats held up by concrete pillars. The benches had fallen apart, and we decided to fix them. Back then we didn't have video games and had to use our imagination and make up games for fun. I suppose we considered ourselves construction workers.

I was told to hold the concrete slabs while the others placed the green slats into the hole to reconstruct the bench.

Here I was, just six years old, trying to support a 200-pound piece of concrete. The concrete slab began to tilt. From this point everything seemed to happen in slow motion. My brother and his friends turned toward me, but they were helpless. Within seconds—but it felt like an eternity—the slab came crashing down on my Keds. Even with all my energy and quickness, I hadn't managed to move my foot fast enough. Andre and Leslie carried me home. It was a hot summer day, and my brother and his friends were sweating even more, wondering what was going to happen to them when they got me back home. This is why Andre didn't want me hanging with him—he would be held accountable. See, the way my mother disciplined us would be considered child abuse today. Let's just say the belt on our behinds was a luxury. We managed to sneak into the house, bypassing the kitchen, dining room, and living room without being noticed by my mother. We were trying to perfectly time when we would tell her that my poor foot had been flattened like a flapjack. I was sitting on the couch, and I had hidden my foot with my black sneaker, now purple and red from the blood seeping through it and onto the side of the sofa. Moms came downstairs. She had been cleaning and had a broom in her hand. This would not have been the opportune time to tell her, but the silence was killing us, and I could hide my bloody leg only so long.

"What the hell happened to your brother, Andre?" she asked.

Before he could finish explaining, she was tearing his butt up with her broom.

My parents took me to Beth Israel Hospital, where a cast

was put on my foot. It was painful at first, but there were some advantages. I got to hang out in my parents' bedroom for a few weeks while everyone waited on me. Best of all, I didn't have to go to school. I just knew this must be what it felt like to be a king.

Before taking me to the hospital, Moms also let Leslie's mother, Mrs. Richardson, know what had happened. He, too, received a beating, courtesy of my foot injury. See, Mrs. Richardson had been in the Army—had even lost an eye during a war—and it was pretty well known that she would literally box her sons whenever they did something wrong.

Carlton tried to latch on to me the way I tried to latch on to Andre. But, like Andre, I wasn't having it. In retrospect, it's probably a good thing that I didn't let him hang with me, especially in my late teen years. Those were tough years in which I did many things that now make me ashamed. But I still regret not spending more time with my baby brother, who probably suffered the most when Pop left. After the divorce, Carlton's grades dropped, and he seemed to lose interest in school. Always a chunky kid, he was the brunt of teasing among kids in the neighborhood. The constant humiliation destroyed his confidence. He was placed in a special-education program at the same high school I attended, and he graduated in 1994. He works infrequently and still lives at home with Moms. But he's a good guy who managed to resist the seduction of drugs and easy money. Given the environment in which he was raised, that is no small accomplishment.

Crack hit the streets of Newark like a cyclone in the 1980s,

and the area around the Dayton Street Projects was swept up
in it. By 1987, my freshman year in high school, drug dealers
were hustling vials of the drug on every street corner. They
were mostly young guys who had either dropped out of
school or lost interest in it and saw a quick way to fill their
pockets with wads of cash, buy expensive gold chains, Nike
and Adidas sneakers, clothes and cars, and attract women
who before had been out of their reach. Violent crimes—
muggings, robberies, carjackings, and murders—skyrock-
eted. Dealers protected their turf with automatic weapons.
Shootouts on the street or playgrounds sometimes sent us
running for cover. A walk to the corner store in broad daylight
might result in a gun pointed to your head and robbery, or
worse. Bullet-riddled bodies found in abandoned stairwells,
and the faces of teenagers on the obituary pages of the newspaper, became the daily toll of what felt like war.

I saw many mothers become crack addicts, hustling their
bodies to stay connected to their new white god. Burglars
broke into our house four times. Each time, they tripped the
lock on the window or the door, entered the house, walked
right over us while we were sleeping, and left the window or
door wide open on their way out. The next morning we discovered belongings missing: a television, a stereo, anything
that could be pawned for quick cash.

Once, when my uncle T.J. and aunt Doretha were visiting,
burglars broke into the basement, where Carlton and I slept,
made it upstairs to the kitchen, and were on their way to the
living room when Uncle T.J., who was sleeping there on a pull-

out sofa, began chasing them. They dashed out of the closest door. He ran outside to his car, got his gun, and chased them down the street. But they managed to get away.

My two best childhood friends, Noody and Will, lived across the street in the projects. So, despite Moms's warnings to stay on my side of the street, I spent all of my free time there. We attended Dayton Street Elementary School, and after school and on weekends we played basketball on its outdoor court. Or we'd play football in open areas of the projects.

One of our favorite games was sponge ball, which is played similar to baseball but with a hard, spongy ball. I would mimic different pros when we played. When I pitched I was Dwight Gooden from the Mets, when I batted I was Don Mattingly or Rickey Henderson. I went so far as to copy those guys' batting stances. Noody, who batted left, would be Darryl Strawberry, who is also a lefty slugger, or Nolan Ryan, a power pitcher with a wicked fastball and an off-pace curveball.

My next-door neighbor, whom we simply knew as Mr. Brown, often watched the two of us playing sponge ball from his window. He had been an avid baseball player in his day and was impressed by our dedication. Once, he even took Noody and me to a Mets game and bought us hot dogs. He didn't know it, but that was my first time attending a professional baseball game. I had the time of my life.

Noody and I both had dreams of someday making it to the majors. When I played on my high school baseball team, the coach told me I was one of his best players. But our sports program was seriously lacking compared to teams in some of the suburbs and surrounding areas. When we played teams from Cedar Grove, Montclair, and Bloomfield, we weren't prepared. Those schools had their own gyms, manicured fields, and dedicated pitching, catching, and field coaches, while we had run-down fields, used equipment, and often not even enough players.

Noody would get to live part of our dream, though. The father of a Hispanic guy who lived in his building took a liking to both of us and asked us to play on his team in the Pony League, where he was a coach. I was fourteen, one year older than the cutoff age, but Noody, who was two years younger, was able to play. It didn't take long for me to see his skills develop. Noody would eventually get a baseball scholarship to Essex Catholic High School and, while I was away at college with George and Rameck, he would land a baseball scholarship at Fairleigh Dickinson University. But unlike me, he was without a built-in support network of friends. Homesick, Noody returned after his freshman year to what he knew, the Dayton Street Projects.

When we were kids, sports saved us many times from the dangers in our neighborhood. We'd play ball behind the school or in the courtyard of the projects while gunshots rang out around the corner. Sometimes, though, the danger unfolded right in front of us.

One day, Noody and I bought a sponge ball from a neighborhood store for a dollar and headed back to the projects to play. We stopped at Building 6, where Noody lived. The fading "X" spray-painted on the wall next to the stairwell marked the strike zone for the pitcher.

As we played, we saw a familiar drug dealer enter the stairwell with a man we didn't recognize. The man wasn't from the neighborhood, which probably meant he was a customer. Seconds after he got inside, another drug dealer sneaked in from behind and began to beat the man with a bat. The two dealers then snatched the man's money and ran. Noody and I watched the whole scene, then went back to playing sponge ball. We had seen it many times before.

The sounds of gunshots and screeching cars late at night and before dawn were as familiar to us as the chirping of insects must be to people who live in the country. In broad daylight we often saw young guys, barely old enough to see over the steering wheel, speeding down Ludlow Street in stolen cars. Sometimes, a trail of speeding police cars would be on their tail.

I was in the sixth grade when I awakened one morning to a loud crash outside. Minutes later, the wail of sirens filled my room. I jumped up and rushed outside. Down the street, about a block from my house, a car had crashed into a utility pole. The pole lay across the smashed front window and hood of the car. As paramedics pulled the driver from the car, I recognized him as a guy who had gone to my school—he was no more than twelve years old. He had been speeding down the street in a stolen car when he lost control. Now he was dead.

This is the backdrop against which I lived. You see it enough, and it becomes normal. Some parts of the life even become exciting. How can a mother's pleas compete with the thrill of having wads of cash handed to you when your pockets are empty and the pantry is bare? Sure, you see cats your age dying all the time, but you figure that's the price you pay for being born poor. And you accept your fate, unless someone or something convinces you that you have the power to change the script.

Even as early as elementary school, the pressure was on me to do what the other neighborhood boys were doing. The pressure was subtle: participate, or feel like a chump and risk being isolated. When I was about seven, the big thing was to run into Jack's, a neighborhood grocery, and steal Icees. My friends were always bragging about how easy it was. I was in the store one sweltering summer day with a friend and decided I wanted a large cherry-flavored Icee, which cost fifty cents. The problem was, I had no money. I opened the freezer, slipped the big, cold cup into my shorts, and walked casually toward the door with my friend. Suddenly, I felt a pair of huge hands on the back of my arm. One of the store's owners, a big, burly Hispanic man over six feet tall, pulled my friend and me to the back of the store.

"Open your pants," he demanded.

"No," I shot back.

He grabbed my shorts and the Icee clunked to the ground. My heart was thumping. I thought for sure I was about to die. The next thing I knew, I was face-to-face with two snarling dogs. They were German shepherds, and they looked big enough to eat me alive. I screamed for mercy. In his thick Spanish accent, the owner was shouting something about letting the dogs tear me to pieces if I ever tried to pull that trick again. I could have sworn the dogs were licking their chops when the owner suddenly let us go. We flew out of the store. I didn't have much of a taste for stolen Icees after that.

But it wouldn't be the last time I followed friends into trouble. It would take years for me to learn that friendship can lift you up, strengthen and empower you, or break you down, weaken and defeat you. In the meantime, though, I kept getting mixed up with neighborhood guys who had lost all hope that their lives would ever be different from what we all saw around us every day.

At thirteen, I was arrested for the first time and charged with shoplifting. A friend set me up. That must sound like the lamest excuse on the books, but it was true. I had walked up Ludlow Street to the Food Town grocery in the bordering city of Elizabeth with a seventeen-year-old friend who told me that he was planning to start a carpet-cleaning business. As we were leaving the store, he said he had paid for a high-powered vacuum cleaner-steamer and needed my help getting it home.

"Grab that for me, man," he said, motioning to a large vacuum cleaner against the wall near the exit. "My hands are full."

We had split up for a few minutes in the store, so it never occurred to me that he was lying. I casually walked over to the machine and pushed it out of the store. I was halfway down the street with it when a police officer rolled up behind me, jumped out of the car, and snapped a pair of handcuffs on me. My friend took off running. I was dumbfounded.

I was detained for a few hours at the Elizabeth police station and then released when the same guy who had been with me in the store and planned the scheme sent his older brother to bail me out. Eventually, the charges were dropped. But the crazy thing is, I kept hanging with the guy who had set me up. I didn't know any better. To my friends, my arrest was one big joke. I never told any of them how scared I was sitting in that police station. That wouldn't have been cool. I just played along. Yeah, man, real funny.

When I look back over my life, I realize that at the most critical stages, someone was there to reach me with exactly what I needed. A martial-arts teacher named Reggie was one of those people. My brother Andre had taken kung fu lessons from Reggie and had introduced me to him when I was ten. Reggie was in his early twenties himself, and he worked as a security guard in the cemetery across the street from my house. I looked up to him. He made an honest living, didn't do drugs, and took good care of himself. He was cool and the only man I knew who was respected by some of the toughest guys in the community for doing good. He was looked up to in that bigger-than-life way more often reserved for drug deal-ers. In Reggie, I saw what I wanted to be: a good guy who commanded respect from the streets in a way that was differ-ent from everything I had seen.

Kung fu was popular at the time. I watched it on television every Saturday morning. Reggie was a highly ranked black belt, good enough to star in a movie, and he taught lessons free of charge at the cemetery to any kid in the neighborhood eager to learn. I never knew anything about Reggie's back-ground, but I wonder now where he got the insight at such a young age to provide a diversion to kids who could so easily drift into trouble.

On Sundays, a small group of us—Lee, Cornell, Crusher, Eric, and some other drifters—walked through huge, mahogany doors and gathered in an empty room that converted to a chapel for memorial services. Reggie worked behind a desk there. Sometimes he wore his security-guard uniform as he led us in practice; other times he practiced with us. We started with warm-up exercises, then spent at least an hour perfecting old sparring moves and learning new ones. Then Reggie led us in meditation. He taught us how to remove ourselves from our environment through deep concentration. As we sat on the floor with our eyes closed and minds blank, Reggie delivered little messages. They were mostly clichés, like "If the blind leads the blind, both of them will fall into a hole." Or, "If you feel weak, you will be weak." But something about sitting there with your mind clear, totally focused on what he was saying, gave his words power.

At the end of each session, we exercised again for an hour, jogging around the cemetery several times or through the neighborhood. We looked like soldiers, jogging in unison with stone faces, right past the tall granite tombstones inside the cemetery gates or the drug dealers and hustlers hanging around outside. The sessions made me feel physically and mentally strong. They had another benefit: they kept me from roaming the streets. I looked up to Reggie and didn't want to disappoint him.

For four years I was dedicated to learning everything I could about martial arts from my mentor-teacher. But by age fifteen, I had started to slip. I was hanging out until one A.M. with guys who were four to seven years older. We sat around drinking forty ounces of malt liquor and talking trash. At first, I just listened as they shared war stories about their dealings around Dayton Street. In time, though, I would have stories of my own.

A year later, I stopped going to kung fu lessons. I'm sure it's no coincidence that about the same time, my life shifted gears and began speeding toward trouble.

No matter how much I hung out with my friends and pretended not to care about school, I always managed to excel. Moms couldn't help me with homework, but she stayed on me to do well.

"Go to school, Marshall," she said so seriously, as if my life depended on it.

I saw close-up how she suffered without an education, and I didn't want the same thing to happen to me. I aimed as far as I could see: finishing high school. Beyond that, I had no ambition. My teachers seemed to like me. As tough as I acted outside school, I paid attention to them in class and usually did what they asked. Sometimes, though, I had to be creative in explaining a good grade to friends. I lied to them frequently. "I cheated," I'd say, trying to minimize any accomplishment. Kids who did well in school were considered nerds. I wanted to be cool. And more than anything, I wanted to fit in.

Moms had placed many of her dreams on me. She had sacrificed her education for her family, and she pushed to make sure I took advantage of the opportunity she never had.

Most students in our neighborhood attended Dayton Street Elementary until the eighth grade, then went on to high school. In the sixth grade, I was looking forward to returning to Dayton Street as a seventh-grader, an upperclassman, running things. But my sixth-grade teacher, Ms. Sandi Schimmel, approached me and recommended that I take an examination to apply to a magnet program at University High School the following year. University High was one of the more prestigious high schools in the Newark school system and the only one that accepted seventh- and eighth-graders.

I didn't want to be bothered with going to another school. Everyone I knew had stayed at Dayton Street until eighth grade.

"Why?" I asked the teacher.

She explained that attending University High would give me a better shot at getting into college and making something of my life. College was far from my mind. But Ms. Schimmel and the principal talked to my mother. They told her that I was reading on a ninth-grade level and needed to be at a school where I would be academically challenged. Moms pushed me to take the test.

It helped that I wasn't the only one handpicked from my school to apply. One of my boys, Craig Jordan, was encouraged to take the test, too. On test day, we rode the bus together to University High School, a boxy two-story structure in the middle of a working-class residential neighborhood. It took us an hour and a half on two public buses to get to the South Ward, where the school was located.

At University High, we walked into a room of unfamiliar faces. George was in the room somewhere, but we would not meet until later. I felt uncomfortable, but practically everybody there was from somewhere else, so we all looked a bit out-of-place. I tried hard to concentrate on the test. It wasn't as difficult as I expected. A few weeks later, I got the news: I had made the cut. I was about to become a student at University High.

# 3

## MA

### *Rameck*

FOR MUCH OF MY CHILDHOOD, my mother and I lived with her mother, Ellen Bradley. She was more than a grandmother to me. She was like my mother, too.

I called her Ma.

She was the steadiest person in my life. But my mother and grandmother didn't get along, and I often felt torn between the two. My mother, Arlene Hunt, was just seventeen, a junior in high school, when I was born. She says she planned the pregnancy in hopes of having a child of her own to love. She blamed Ma for an unhappy childhood and as a teenager turned to drugs—first marijuana, then heroin, then cocaine, then sleeping pills—to dull her pain. Slowly, her addiction transformed her from the ambitious, loving, attentive mother I adored into a needy woman I struggled to forgive. My father was a heroin addict, too, and he spent most of my early years in jail, doing time for petty crimes he committed to support his habit.

Ma's house was where I felt most secure.

Ma grew up in Newark and at sixteen married my mother's father, Raymond Hunt, a fair-skinned, half-Jewish man known around town as "Sugar Shoes" because he always sported the latest in crocodile, alligator, or lizard skin on his feet. My mother was a "daddy's girl," the second-oldest of four children the couple had together—Raymond, my mother, Richard, and Venus. But Mom was just a toddler when her parents divorced. Ma began dating a truck driver named Theodore Green, her on-again, off-again live-in companion until his death in 1979. He was the father of Ma's three youngest children—Sheldon, Victoria, and Nicole.

The family lived in Newark until the summer of 1971, when the state offered families money to relocate if they lived in the path of a planned new state highway, Route 78. To Ma it was a blessing from God, a chance to provide a better life for her children. She found a nice, two-story house on Clinton Avenue, a busy residential street in Plainfield, about eighteen miles away. Back then, the neighborhood was mixed, with mostly working-class white, Irish Catholic, and black families. But over the next two decades, as I was growing up, my grandmother's community would become nearly indistinguishable from Newark, as white families fled, poor black and Latino families moved in, and drug dealers crossed the borders.

Our house had three bedrooms, a bathroom, a living room, a dining room, a kitchen, a full basement, and a sun porch that Ma converted into another bedroom. To my mother, then fifteen, the move from a bustling city to a boring suburb was devastating. As the oldest girl, she bore most of the responsibility of caring for her five younger siblings while Ma worked. She began dating my father and soon began trying to get pregnant so she could return to Newark to attend an evening high school for pregnant girls. It worked—at least for a while. When she got pregnant with me, my mother moved back to Newark to care for a cousin's children during the day and attend the special school in the evenings. But when I was born, we returned to Plainfield to Ma's house, where her five younger siblings still lived. Uncle Raymond, who later joined the Nation of Islam and changed his named to Rahman Shabazz, had moved out and was living on his own.

We shared bedrooms and fought for time in the bathroom. On Friday nights, Ma and her older children sat around the kitchen table and played cards—poker, spades, and tonk—often for money, all night long. Ma loved playing cards. Sometimes her friends came over for all-night card games around the kitchen table. Beer flowed, music played in the background, cards slapped against the table, and laughter filled the room. I would perch somewhere in the kitchen to watch, too young to join in the fun. We also had family tournaments of Monopoly. And on Sunday, Ma cooked huge country dinners—turkey, dressing, collard greens, cornbread, macaroni and cheese, and sweet-potato pie. Even as her children grew older and began moving out, Ma still cooked those big Sunday dinners that drew everybody back to the house.

I was the designated family entertainer. My aunts and uncles loved to watch me dance. They'd gather around me in the middle of the living-room floor as I showed off my latest moves. They would clap, laugh, bob their heads to the beat of the music, and shower praise on me. I was just four or five, and I craved the attention.

I was in preschool when my mother and I moved out for the first time. Mom had gotten a job at Bell Laboratories in 1976 and was earning enough money to make it on her own. She found an apartment, which she decorated and kept meticulously. I had my own room with a Mickey Mouse telephone and all the latest toys. She and I went everywhere together; when I was six, we even traveled to Disney World with one of her girlfriends. Those were the happiest days I ever spent with my mother.

One night, as Mom and I were watching the Miss America pageant, I turned from the television screen to her.

"Mom, why don't you try out for that?" I asked. "You're prettier than all those girls."

She was, of course, flattered. I was quite serious. I thought my mom was the prettiest woman I had ever seen. She was slim and shapely with honey-colored skin and dark brown hair that flowed down her back and matched her dark eyes. Men loved her.

Mom was young and still loved to party. She sometimes hosted parties at our apartment on Saturday nights. When she sent me to my room, I could hear the laughter of her friends mixing with the soulful sounds of the top '70s jams. A few times when I sneaked a peek into the living room, I saw my mom and her friends dancing or chilling in the haze of an odd-smelling cigarette. I realize now that it was marijuana.

Mom left Bell Labs in 1980 and moved from job to job. By the time I enrolled in first grade, we were moving around a lot. Mom began having trouble paying the bills, so we moved from one apartment to another or back to Ma's house. I attended a different elementary school every year, except in third and fourth grades. But I was always a smart, curious kid who made good grades without much effort. In the second grade, I scored high enough on a placement test to enter the Plainfield public-school system's "gifted and talented" program.

A big component of the program took place after school. A bus would pick us up from various elementary schools that participated and transport us to the local middle school, where we received several hours of academic enrichment. The director of the program, a kindhearted woman in her forties named Mrs. Hatt, seemed to take a special interest in me. All of the kids in the program were smart, but she always singled me out for praise—or, at least, I thought I was being singled out. Maybe she pulled other kids aside, too, and said nice things, but she made me feel special.

"You know, Rameck, you are so smart," she would say, as though she were telling me something that was just between us. "You really are gifted."

She said it so often that I started to think, well, maybe I was. She taught us science and how to use a computer—in the early days when few schools had computers. The weirdest thing sticks out in my mind about her: she taught me how to spell and define the word "hypothesis."

No matter which public elementary school I attended in Plainfield, I remained in the program through the eighth grade, except for the third and fourth grades, when I attended Catholic school. As I grew older, I always complained about not having any money, so Mrs. Hatt began inviting me to her house to help her in the garden. I think she just wanted to put a few dollars in my pockets because I never did more than pull up a few weeds.

I was surprised to learn that she lived in Plainfield in a neighborhood not too far from Ma's. I thought all the white people had moved out by then. She was married to an artist, and their house had a stucco face with a long garage and huge front and back yards. Inside was filled with expensive-looking sculptures and framed art. I remember looking around the house with wide eyes, thinking, "I want a house like this someday."

Despite my mother's drug use, she always pushed me to excel. When I brought home my report card, she let me know that she expected A's. In her mind, a C was failure. Ma thought she was too tough on me. But Mom argued: "My son ain't settling for no C." Most of the time I did as well as she expected. I wanted to please her. But I also knew better than to fail. My mom didn't play when it came to school, and I knew I would get a serious butt-whuppin' if I brought home bad grades.

As difficult as our relationship eventually became, I always knew she wanted me to have the best. She aspired to be middle-class, and she was determined to have fine clothes and furniture and a child in private school, even it meant living well above her means. When I was in the third grade, she enrolled me in St. Mary's Catholic School, where she thought I would get a better education—although, knowing my mother, I'm sure she enjoyed telling people she had a son in private school. But my class spent much of the year on tasks I had learned the year before in public school. I started misbehaving in class. My behavior was so disruptive that the teacher recommended I be placed in special education. But my mother wasn't about to let that happen. Her son in special education? Hell, no! I was too smart for that, she argued. I just wasn't being challenged. She won that battle, but after the fourth grade, she moved me back to public school, where I returned to the "gifted and talented" program.

I always longed to be close to my father. So even when he was in jail, my mother took me to visit him. He went to jail three different times for stints of eighteen months to two years. I was just one year old in 1974 when he was sentenced for the first time.

I thought jail was where my father lived. When I visited him there, we mostly spent time in a picnic area behind the jail. We sat across from each other on wooden benches and posed for pictures together as though we were in his backyard. It didn't seem abnormal because many of my friends' fathers were in jail, too.

This was far from how my father's life had begun.

He was born in October 1953 outside Wilmington, North Carolina, the oldest boy of six children Fred and Winnie Jones had together. They gave him his father's name, Fred Howard Jones. In 1960, Fred and Winnie moved their family to Newark to find work. My grandfather worked in printing shops, and my grandmother found jobs in various factories. Years later, she enrolled in college and became a registered nurse.

I've always admired my grandmother for that. The two of us would grow close in high school when I bought a car and was old enough to drive myself to visit her. Later, I sometimes stayed at her house during breaks from college.

Like Ma, my paternal grandmother taught me a lot about the importance of family. Many times I saw her give her last dollar to make sure her children and grandchildren had what they needed. My father is a lot like her in that way. When I was in college, she used to say, "No matter what you do in life, it's gonna be hard, so you might as well do something positive. At least you can reap the benefits in the end." She was absolutely right. Some of my old friends who were drug dealers used to tell me that they felt stress all the time, worrying about getting robbed, going to jail, even dying. School was hard, but at least it would pay off someday.

When my father was growing up, his family lived on Prince Street, across the street from the Stella Wright Projects where George grew up. It was one of Newark's toughest neighborhoods, but his parents placed him in private schools: Queen of Angels Elementary and Essex Catholic High School. He took college-preparatory courses and maintained a high-B average. When he graduated in 1971, he snagged an academic scholarship to Assumption College in Worcester, Massachusetts. He was one of just a handful of black students on campus, and he had a difficult time adjusting. This was the 1970s, that life-defining time in American history when black students throughout the country were growing Afros, throwing their fists into the air, and listening to the fiery rhetoric of leaders like Stokely Carmichael. Dad felt isolated from the movement at a school where so few others looked and thought like him. But he planned to major in chemistry and earned a 3.5 grade-point average in the first semester.

My parents were introduced by a childhood friend of my father's when he returned from college for Christmas break. Dad had been a popular basketball player in high school, and my mother, still a high-school student, was a cheerleader at a different school from the one he had attended. They began dating, but my mother didn't know that my father was already dating a cheerleader at another nearby high school. Both girls got pregnant around the same time, and my half-sister, Quamara, and I were born in 1973, just eighteen days apart.

Everything changed for my father, though, while he was visiting a friend during the same Christmas break. When he walked into the apartment, all of his friends were getting high. Someone offered him heroin, and he accepted, desperately wanting to be part of the in-crowd.

From the day he took that first shot of heroin, my dad was hooked. He began to shoot up whenever and wherever he could. He returned to Assumption College the following semester in January, but he got into a fight with a group of white guys, dropped out of college, and returned to Newark.

He enrolled in the Army but was discharged after two years when he was arrested for committing a robbery while on furlough. There were long periods during which he managed to function and hold a decent job while still dependent on drugs. But it would take him twenty-six years to conquer the addiction that drained him of any ambition beyond life on the streets. In 1997, after many attempts at rehabilitation, he left

Newark and entered two different out-of-state rehabilitation programs back-to-back and began to turn his life around. He returned to Newark but to a different life. He now works at a drug rehabilitation center as a counselor.

When I was fourteen, Dad noticed that my life seemed headed in a similar direction to his, and he tried to intervene. I wasn't using drugs, but I was hanging out with guys who, like me, were lost and acting like little thugs, trying to define our manhood by wild, foolish behavior. My father was not yet clean, but he tried to reach me. He told me he wanted my life to be better than his. He said drugs and jail were not the life he had planned for himself. He had just gotten sucked in and couldn't find his way out. He told me he was living a lie and was tired of watching his friends die around him.

"Don't let the same thing happen to you," he pleaded.

His words touched me, but I was hardheaded. It would take a short stint in juvenile jail at age sixteen for me to realize finally that I was following my friends to a place of self-destruction.

I'm not sure when I began to suspect that my mother was abusing drugs. I just pieced together the signs on my own. I was eleven when my mother had a second child, my little sister, Mecca, whose father lived with us sometimes. But like most of the men in my mother's life, he didn't seem to be good for her. He, too, ended up behind bars. The stress of now having two little mouths to feed must have been too much for my mother. Mom was without work for a while, and we went on welfare. The bills went unpaid more often. We spent days at a time in apartments with no lights, air conditioning, or heat when the utility company turned off our electricity. I learned how to twist my little sister's hair in ponytails, and I made sure she had something to eat, even if I had to call relatives for help.

Many nights, I cried myself to sleep. I tried to strike a deal with God.

"God, please, just get one of my parents off drugs," I prayed.

I figured asking Him to save them both would be too much. I swore I would never use drugs.

My mother's drug habit messed up everything. But the thing that hurt me most was that it robbed her of something I always thought came naturally: a mother's instinct. The kind of instinct that makes a mother dash into the path of a speeding car or rush into a burning building to rescue her endangered child. The kind of instinct that makes a child feel protected. When my mother's drug abuse got out of control, I no longer felt protected.

I was about thirteen when my mother told me that she used drugs. She said she needed them to help her deal with her pain. She had many unfulfilled dreams. In high school, she had wanted to become a court stenographer. It seemed like such an important job, and it intrigued her. But she had gotten pregnant and never pursued it. After graduating from high school in 1974, she'd studied business administration intermittently at Essex County College for about a year and a half, but she never finished. Later, she also told me that when she was a child, a relative had molested her.

My emotions toward her swung from pity to anger and back again.

At times, my mother accused me of loving my father more than I loved her. That wasn't true. I did, however, feel less anger toward him. It is true that my mother struggled in part because my father didn't always do his share to support me financially. Yet I blamed her for leaving me without a shield. Perhaps I was angrier at her because I loved her so much and I wondered whether she loved me back. I couldn't help suspecting that she loved the drugs more.

I never questioned my father's love. If I asked him for help, he never turned me away if he had it to give. If I happened to find him on his way to buy drugs and said, "Dad, I really need five dollars," he'd give it to me. He may have been itching and scratching because he needed a fix so badly, and he may have had only $10 in his pocket. But he would pull it out and give me half. He might lie and say he had to keep the other half for food, and he might leave me and go steal some meat from a grocery store to sell and make up the half he gave me. But through a child's eyes, I saw a father sacrificing his needs for his son's.

At thirteen, I got my first job, sweeping hair from the floor of Bill's Barbershop in Plainfield. I made just $20 a week, but I saved my money to help buy the things I needed, such as school clothes. Eventually, my mother completely stopped buying my clothes. She had no money and too many bills, she said. And besides, I was working and could take care of that myself. She wanted me to be a man. So, at thirteen, I was on my own.

When I needed someone to hear my frustration, I turned to Ma.

"It's gonna be all right," she always said.

Ma comforted me when I needed it, but she refused to baby me. She believed it was a good thing that I had to work and take care of myself. It taught me responsibility, she said. And she rarely gave me money.

Ma was a hardworking woman who didn't believe in waste. She was still young, just thirty-seven, when I was born. I never saw her sick, and I never saw her cry. She rose every morning at four A.M., drank a cup of coffee in the kitchen, smoked a cigarette, and headed to her job at the post office in Newark. She drove a red Caprice Classic. I loved that car because it was so comfortable.

My grandmother was, without a doubt, the head of her household. But she always told me that a woman should make her man feel as though he is in charge, even if she is running things. After Theodore Green's death, Ma met and married a man we all called Hook. He walked with a limp and was unable to work. He collected some kind of check for his disability and drank heavily. When he was drunk, he was kinder to me, often peeling off crisp bills, $10 and $20 at a time from the wad he kept in his pocket. But he usually kept to himself, preferring to watch television in his room rather than participate in our family card and board games.

While visiting Ma once, I found an old, frayed black-and-white picture of her when she was a teenager. She was stunning—slender with smooth, dark-brown skin and long hair the color of coal. Ma had aged with grace, growing a bit thicker with the years. She lost much of her hair and wore short, curly brown wigs over her own graying, braided locks.

Ma was religious, though she didn't go to church much. She prayed at home, read her Bible regularly, and was quick to remind you what the good Lord said. When family members had problems, they came to Ma to fix them. She gave good advice, always straight-up and sometimes tough to swallow.

As a working teenager, I always wanted to buy the newest and most expensive sneakers to keep up with my friends.

"Look, you don't have that kind of money," Ma told me bluntly. "You don't have a pot to piss in, nor a window to throw it out. Don't try to live high off the hog."

What usually followed was a winding tale about the good old days when she was a girl and owned just two pairs of pants and two shirts and had to wash—by hand, no less—one of the outfits every night to have clean clothes to wear the next day. That was the last thing I wanted to hear, but even now when I'm tempted to splurge, I hear Ma's voice: *Don't try to live high off the hog.*

In junior high school, I began acting in plays. I was in the seventh grade when I first joined the cast of *The Wiz* with a friend to be close to some pretty girls. My friend got a major role, the Lion, while I only got to play the gatekeeper. The next year, I auditioned and got to play a main character in an original play written by a woman we knew as Miss Scott, who lived in New York and was the friend of the school's chorus teacher. The cast did so well that we traveled to Atlanta and performed the play for seven different schools. The applause from the audience was thrilling. It was the most incredible feeling I had ever felt. I began thinking about acting as a career.

Miss Scott was so impressed with her young actors that she decided to start an acting school in New York. I enrolled and caught a train to New York every Saturday morning to study acting with her. My mother said she didn't have the money to pay for the lessons, but Miss Scott liked me so much she allowed me to attend anyway.

"Don't worry about it," she said. "We'll work something out."

Later, Miss Scott explained that each of us needed a portfolio to land acting roles, and she arranged for a photographer to take our pictures. The session would cost $150. I didn't have it. I asked Ma for help. She and one of my aunts agreed to give me the money. But Ma warned me to leave the money at her house and pick it up the next morning on my way to New York. She feared my mother would either take it or make up a sob story and I would give it to her.

Ma believed in tough love. She told me that my mother would never realize that she needed professional help as long as we constantly bailed her out.

I took the money home anyway. As soon as I walked in the door, I realized we had no electricity. My mother was upset.

"What am I going to do?" she kept asking, as if I had some magical solution.

She had gone grocery shopping earlier in the week, and the refrigerator and freezer were full of food. She was afraid the food would spoil.

"You got any money?" she asked me.

At first, I lied. I wanted the pictures for my portfolio so badly, and I knew the money in my pocket was my only shot at getting them. I wouldn't be able to go back to Ma again if I gave her hard-earned money away.

Guilt began nipping at my conscience. My baby sister wasn't quite two years old, and she needed cold milk. Her milk would spoil without electricity to keep the refrigerator cold. And how happy would I be with my portfolio if my sister went hungry even a day because I was too selfish to help my mother?

I gave up the money.

The same night, we moved the food in the refrigerator and freezer to a neighbor's house. It was late Friday evening, too late for the utility company to restore power to the apartment, my mother said. We endured the weekend without power. But she held on to my money.

Three or four days later, she returned the $150, but Ma now wanted her money back. She was angry at me for defying her. But she also wanted me to understand that there are times when I have to put my needs first.

"You can't help nobody 'til you help yourself," she said.

I had to learn a tough lesson.

I never got the pictures for my portfolio. For that, I blamed my mother.

That was the last year I lived with her. We weren't getting along. She tried to be strict with me, requiring me to be in by nine P.M. and always fussing about my grades. But I had little respect for her because I knew she was using drugs. I began skipping school and getting into fights while hanging out with my friends. Mom worried that my troubles would escalate if I went to Plainfield High School with them. She had instilled in me as far back as I can remember the idea that I had to go to college.

But I wasn't thinking about college when my mother came in and announced unexpectedly one summer day that I would be attending University High School in Newark in the fall. She had confided her fears to her godmother, who was an assistant principal at University High. Unbeknownst to me, the two women had enrolled me at University High for ninth grade. When my mother told me what she had done, I was furious. I wanted to go with my boys to Plainfield High School.

As far as my mother was concerned, that wasn't an option.

I moved to Newark to live with an uncle who had a spare room.

I met Sam and George my first day at University High. We took the same Advanced Placement courses. I was one of the few AP students who hadn't attended University High in the seventh and eighth grades, and I stood out as the new kid.

Sam and George were already friends. I'd see them together at lunch, and we were all cordial to one another. Gradually, we started talking more, and they seemed like two smart, cool guys. But for a while, I clung to my boys in Plainfield.

In my sophomore year, my uncle moved, and I had to find another place to stay. I lived temporarily with my father, his girlfriend, her son Mike, and my sister Daaimah, then moved back to Ma's house in Plainfield. Ma never closed her doors to me.

In the mornings, I rode to school with one of my teachers, Miss Ransom, who lived in Plainfield and picked me up at

Ma's house. She was one of the coolest teachers at University High. She was a no-nonsense kind of instructor, and I trusted her. When I later got into trouble with the law, she was one of the few people I told. I was always getting into some mischief at school, and that really baffled her.

"Rameck, you're such a smart guy," she said during our drive. "Why do you act this way?"

In the afternoons, I rode the bus to the Newark post office and waited for Ma's shift to end at three-thirty P.M. We rode home together.

When I think back to some of my favorite moments with Ma, I remember those days, cruising in that red Caprice Classic, just the two of us, sharing tidbits from our day. She seemed to understand my struggles—the heartbreak I felt about my parents' addictions, the confusion I felt about my own blossoming manhood, and the pull I felt from my friends. Like other family members, she tried gently to warn me.

"Don't let the wrong group of friends influence you," she said.

I wish I had listened. But that was another of Ma's lessons that I had to learn the hard way.

# 4

## COMMON GROUND

### *George*

SOMETIMES PEOPLE ARE drawn together for a purpose that even they don't recognize at the time. I am convinced that this is what happened with Sam, Rameck, and me.

Almost as soon as Sam and I met in the seventh grade, we realized we liked the same things: baseball, basketball, video games, Nike sneakers, and the latest fashions in clothes. We did our work in school, but we weren't nerds. We didn't allow school to consume us. It seemed that most students were either so smart that they had little or no social skills, or they were so sociable that they goofed off during class and neglected their schoolwork. I tended to lean toward people who offered a balance. That's what I saw in Sam. He and I often ended up sitting next to each other, learning lessons together, sharing candy and stories about our lives and the happenings in our neighborhoods.

All of the seventh- and eighth-graders at University High School had been recommended by a teacher, guidance counselor, or principal at our elementary schools and had been required to pass a test for admittance. University High, one of Newark's three magnet high schools, had earned a solid reputation for sending a high percentage of its graduates to colleges and universities each year. The school boasts an 85- to 90-percent rate of its graduates completing college in four or five years.

The school grew out of research in the late 1960s that indicated that many of the public school system's graduates were academically unprepared to accept jobs beyond menial labor. Corporations were complaining that they were having trouble meeting new federal guidelines for hiring more minority workers. To respond to the crisis, in 1969 the Newark system initiated a magnet program called "School Within a School" at Southside High School, which later became Malcolm X Shabazz High School. Students considered gifted were separated from the general population there and provided with a more rigorous college-preparatory curriculum.

In 1976, the program leased a building, relocated, and became the school that is now known as University High School. Two years later, it became the only public high school in Newark to begin admitting seventh- and eighth-graders. Administrators had found that students entering in the ninth grade weren't getting the background they needed to prepare them for college in four years. Every year since, the school has selected top seventh-graders from the city's elementary schools and started them early with college-preparatory courses that, by the eighth grade, include algebra, honors English, and a foreign language, often Latin.

The school moved to 55 Clinton Place, its current location, in 1982. The predominantly black neighborhood around the school is mostly working-class, but there are pockets of high-crime areas that have caused problems for students over the years. The blocks around Hawthorne Avenue were the worst. If you weren't ready to fight when you walked around there, you risked getting mugged. Students regularly got robbed of their sneakers, jackets, and bus cards on the way to school or home. I rode the bus to and from school every day, but I went in the opposite direction.

By the end of the seventh grade, Sam and I had become pretty good friends and were hanging out regularly during lunch. We played basketball, sat outside under the trees and played cards, or just sat in the cafeteria, banged out a beat on the table, and rapped.

I was also tight with Faith Evans, now a well-known pop singer, who had attended Spencer Elementary with me. She was mature for her age—too mature to have any interest in me beyond "little brother." Even then she was beautiful, and she dated guys who were at least three years older. She often shared her boyfriend business with me and sought advice, but, given my limited experience with girls at the time, I could only offer a sympathetic ear.

In the evenings after school, I spent hours playing video games with my neighborhood friend Shahid Jackson or football in the apartment-complex parking lot with some of the other guys on the block. Within three blocks of the apartment complex where I lived, there were at least fifteen guys around my age. We broke into cliques, with two different groups doing things I just wasn't willing to do: they sold drugs, stole cars, beat up guys outside their circle, and caused all kinds of havoc in the neighborhood. The rest of us hung out together and avoided the troublemakers, though sometimes we all got together for football.

I didn't know it then, but Sam was having a more difficult time staying away from trouble. His friends tended to be older and more influential. With his engaging personality, Sam has always attracted lots of friends. His loyalty was tested on a regular basis, and in his neighborhood he had to fight to prove that he could walk the streets without being intimidated. Though he was always friendly, you got the feeling there was more going on inside his head than he let on. He held it all inside. I'm quieter, more reserved. I'm not shy, just a laid-back, take-me-as-I-am-or-leave-me kind of guy. In some ways, I think that this protected me. Maybe the troublemakers figured I didn't have the heart to hang with them. I don't know. I just know they didn't bother me. They didn't try to persuade me to join them, and they didn't try to make my life miserable by picking on me.

Sam and I participated in our first graduation ceremony together after completing the eighth grade. Rameck arrived the next year, but Sam and I didn't become close friends with him until our junior year.

University High had a strong math-and-science bent. It offered summer and weekend programs, underwritten by oil and chemical companies interested in producing more engineers, scientists, and mathematicians. We participated in some of those programs, but quite frankly, high school wasn't as challenging as the seventh and eighth grades had been. We had a few dedicated teachers at the high school who pushed us to learn and forced us to do our work, but too many others just didn't know how to reach us and didn't seem to care. They expected and accepted mediocrity or less, and unfortunately, we usually gave no more.

"I got mine. Now you got to get yours," exasperated teachers often told us.

I no longer felt challenged, and my academic performance began to slip. I made average grades, but I could have done better if I had worked harder. Sam, who had graduated Number Three in our eighth-grade class, also dropped to average performance. Rameck made all A's and B's in our freshman year, but his grades dropped, too, in later years. All three of us began to skip classes. It was a common practice among students at our school. We knew we could get away with it, and we did.

Rameck was quiet and low-key during our freshman year. He was still learning his way around his new school. He remained close to his friends in Plainfield and spent time with them. During lunch and between classes, I saw him hanging out with guys who rode the bus with him from his uncle's neighborhood. His two neighborhood buddies didn't return for our sophomore year, and Rameck became friends with two other guys, Hasaan and Ahi, the son of acclaimed poet and human-rights activist Amiri Baraka.

Rameck also had a wild side. He and friends from his old

neighborhood were getting into fights with other boys, and he was always into some kind of mischief. But Rameck was very smart, especially in science and math. He would be cutting up in class one minute and then ace a test that practically everybody else had failed the next. Very few new students were able make it in the Advanced Placement courses at University High if they hadn't attended junior high school there. Rameck was one of the few. He also had an activist spirit and a heart to help people. He was the first to protest an injustice, and he questioned everything. Our instructors never would have guessed that for most of high school Rameck wanted to be a teacher.

Rameck became popular pretty quickly by acting in school plays. In the ninth grade, he won the starring role of Scrooge in a play based on the Charles Dickens classic *A Christmas Carol.* This was a huge upset, because he'd ousted an older guy who captured the lead role in the school play each year. Rameck was later cast as the father in Lorraine Hansberry's play *A Raisin in the Sun.*

As a sophomore, Rameck joined Hasaan and Ahi in forming a group called the United Students Organization (USO) at our school. Ahi shared many of his father's views about self-preservation, self-reliance, and community organization. That appealed to Rameck, who had grown up around uncles who belonged to the Nation of Islam. Students from several Newark public schools belonged to USO, which began to meet at Essex County College to plan strategies for improving the schools. Sam and I attended meetings every now and then, but Rameck was one of the leaders. Eventually, the meetings moved to the basement of the Baraka home.

The group attracted the most attention in our junior year when it organized a student walkout and overnight sit-in at the Board of Education to demand a multicultural curriculum and to protest state budget cuts in education financing. Despite a student population that was overwhelmingly black and Hispanic, public high schools in Newark did not offer classes that taught our history.

On a cool morning in April 1990, hundreds of students walked out of class and spilled into the streets in front of and alongside the school. We boarded public buses headed to Military Park. Along the way, the buses grew more crowded as students from Shabazz, Central, and other high schools joined the protest. From Military Park, we marched to the Newark Board of Education headquarters. We locked arms and chanted. Cars honked as we completely blocked traffic. Police showed up and tried to stop us because we didn't have a permit, but we kept marching. What were they going to do? Beat us, sic their dogs on us, and throw us in jail, as police down South had done to the civil-rights protesters of the 1960s?

It was one of few times when students from rival high schools came together for a useful purpose. When we made it to the board office, police and security guards were standing in front of the door to block our entrance. Our leaders demanded to speak to the superintendent, but the crowd of students grew impatient and we began pushing our way inside. Police arrested Hasaan and Ahi. Students took over the lobby. We sat in rows on the floor. Executive School Superintendent Eugene Campbell eventually came out and addressed us. He also summoned Assemblyman Willie Brown and State Senator Wynona Lipman, who spoke to us. Hours passed. At lunchtime, Superintendent Campbell had sandwiches, milk, and juice handed out to us. By nightfall, many students, including Sam and I, had left. We had to go to our part-time jobs. But a few parents, supportive of our cause, brought blankets and pillows. School officials ordered a pizza dinner for the remaining students. Rameck was among the fifty or so students who spent the night at the board's headquarters.

In the weeks afterward, a committee of parents, students, and educators met to develop a curriculum that included African-American studies and the history of other minority groups. The next year, University High offered a course in African-American and Hispanic history.

As one of the leaders of the protest, Rameck realized that school administrators would probably be watching him closely, and he began to attend classes more regularly. But his mischievous side still surfaced from time to time. One of his practical jokes almost got him kicked out of University High for good.

Rameck didn't like his biology teacher, so he often skipped her class. When he skipped class one day, he decided to return to play a prank on her. He knocked on her door, and when she opened it, he was standing there with a can of Silly String. Without saying a word, he sprayed a web of the colorful, sticky stuff up, down, and across her face and dashed away.

When she turned to face her class, the students burst out laughing. The teacher was humiliated and furious. The principal summoned Rameck to the office and suspended him indefinitely. The superintendent of the Newark public school system banned him from University High School. The teacher told authorities that she had had an allergic reaction to the spray, and she threatened to file criminal charges against Rameck. The incident was the talk of the school.

During his appeal hearing before the superintendent, Rameck pleaded for another chance. He apologized to the teacher, who was sitting in the room. He said he didn't mean to harm her and promised never to do anything like that again. He presented supportive letters from another teacher at the school and from Amiri Baraka. He also had an unexpected ally that day: the offended teacher.

When Rameck finished his presentation, she addressed the superintendent softly.

"Don't kick him out of the school for that," she said. "Let him come back."

Rameck never knew what changed her mind. But she didn't file charges, and the superintendent lifted the suspension, allowing Rameck to return to school.

Rameck could be a real hothead and prankster, but I liked him. I could see even then that he was a really good guy.

Sam and Rameck became friends first. They were among the few students who owned cars in our junior and senior years, and owning a car in high school made you instantly popular. All the girls wanted to date you, and all the guys wanted to be your friend. That's part of what initially drew them together. Rameck owned a Mitsubishi Cordia and Sam an Audi 5000, a cool car mentioned in many rap songs at the time. They often got together on Friday nights and weekends for parties and dates. Sam picked me up sometimes, and I got to know Rameck through him.

I didn't party as much as the two of them did back then, and I didn't drink anything stronger than soda. They drank, but one of the things I really liked about them was that they never hassled me or tried to push me to drink. I could be myself with them.

All three of us worked part-time. Sam and Rameck worked at McDonald's. I stocked shelves at Murray's Steaks in my freshman year, cooked pizza at Chuck E. Cheese my sophomore year, and sold chocolate-chip cookies at Mrs. Fields my senior year.

Sam and I were really into baseball and played on the school's baseball team all four years of high school. Sam played shortstop and pitcher and was co-captain of the team, while I played first base. Since Rameck was hanging out with us now, he wanted to try out for the team, too, but he had never played before. Sam and I agreed to teach him. One day after school, Sam drove us to a park so Rameck could practice batting against a pitching machine. We talked him through the game and showed him how to swing the bat. Rameck took his place in the batting cage. The machine pitched the ball. Rameck swung with all his might. He missed. A second ball shot out. He swung again and missed again. A third ball came. He missed that one, too. The balls kept coming, and Rameck kept missing. We urged him to hold the bat this way or that.

Nothing helped. Sam and I doubled over in laughter as our friend swung futilely at those flying balls. Finally, Rameck quit.

"I'm better at playing girls than baseball," he said. "So, I'll just stick with what I know."

Just before the baseball season in my senior year, I broke my leg. I had been playing basketball with some friends and made a wrong move, and my leg snapped. I still went to practice to watch, and Sam drove out of his way every day to drop me off at home for the entire time that I wore a cast.

The more the three of us hung out, the more we realized how much we had in common. We had long conversations about our families and the crazy things we'd witnessed in our neighborhoods. We also talked about school, what grades we'd made on a certain test, which teachers we liked and disliked, and what we wanted to do with our lives. It was clear that, like me, Sam and Rameck wanted to make something of their lives, even though all three of us were still fuzzy about what careers we wanted to pursue. Though he gave his teachers a hard time, Rameck wanted to be a teacher. He wanted to reach boys like himself, who seemed tough and incorrigible on the outside but really just needed guidance. A counselor had suggested that Rameck consider engineering because he was so good in math and science. At first, the only college he was seriously considering was Howard University in Washington, D.C., where his other two buddies, Hasaan and Ahi, were planning to go.

Sam talked about becoming a businessman, but he never mentioned going to college until our senior year. No one in his family had ever gone to college, and he didn't really think it was an option for him. Over the years I had considered at least a dozen other professions. One minute it was nursing, the next some kind of lab technician. But then, unexpectedly, my old dream was revived.

When our teacher told us that a recruiter from Seton Hall University was going to give a presentation in the library, she gave us a choice: either stay in class or go to the presentation.

The three of us didn't really feel like staying in class. Out in the halls, we concocted an alternative plan. We would walk down the hall as though we were headed to the library, then sneak over to the gym. We were old pros at it by then.

A teacher must have sniffed out our little scheme, because somehow—and to this day I don't remember exactly how—we ended up in the library. Sam, Rameck, and I sat at a back table. As the session opened, we were goofing off, only half-listening.

First, the recruiter tried to sell us on the university's basketball team, which happened to be playing well that year, 1990. I love basketball, but I didn't intend to play in college and wasn't really moved by her spiel. Then she began to talk about the lack of minorities in the health profession. She said Seton Hall was dedicated to training more minority students to enter medicine as doctors through a program that provided free tutoring, counseling, and other support.

My ears tuned in.

The Pre-Medical/Pre-Dental Plus Program was—and still is—one of several initiatives under the umbrella of the Educational Opportunity Program created at Seton Hall in 1968, when black communities in Newark and other cities across the nation were rioting for civil and human rights. The EOP was designed to make higher education possible for poor students who have the ability to succeed in college but are undereducated and would probably be eliminated during the normal college-admissions process.

The EOP finances dozens of specialized programs that provide money for tuition and housing, counseling, tutoring, assessment testing, and more to hundreds of needy students. The state added the Pre-Medical/Pre-Dental Plus Program under the EOP in 1980 because so few minority students were becoming doctors.

The program accepts students based on high-school academic records, teacher recommendations, and personal interviews. SAT scores are considered, but they matter less than in the normal admissions process.

Until that moment, when I heard about the program from the recruiter, I had no real plan. I knew I was going to college. That was it. But this program seemed to lay out all the steps for me.

I could hardly believe my ears. I thought to myself: *Free college. Free tutoring. Help getting into dental school. This is it! This is the way to do what I've always wanted to do.*

I lingered a few minutes in the library to talk to Sam and Rameck. I could tell right away that I was more excited about the program than they were. They were my boys, and I thought it would be cool for us to go to college together.

"What did you think of what the lady said?" I asked.

"It was all right," one of them responded.

"Man, I think I want to do this," I added. "Why don't we go ahead and do this together?"

Of the three of us, Rameck was always the most skeptical, so, as expected, he was reluctant to commit. He didn't want to bother with all the paperwork, he said. Besides, he already had plans to go with two other friends to Howard University in Washington, D.C.

Sam, always the analyst, wasn't interested in spending eight years in school. It seemed like such a long time to him. He was so good with numbers that he always remembered telephone numbers without writing them down and could do long mathematical problems in his head, and he felt he had the head and personality for business. But he had no idea how to become a businessman, and he didn't know anyone in the field who could help him develop those talents.

I was the only one who had ever even thought of becoming a doctor before that day. The truth is, none of us had seen anything to make us believe it was really possible. Sometimes, though, you just have to step out there and believe in something you can't quite see. And something deep down was telling me this was one of those times.

"Man, we could go to college for free," I emphasized.

What did we have to lose by applying?

"Let's do this," I said in as persuasive a voice as I could muster.

Finally, they gave in.

We would apply to Seton Hall, go to college together, then go to medical school and stick with one another to the end.

We didn't lock hands in some kind of empty, symbolic gesture. Nor did we think much further ahead, like what would happen if one of us got accepted and the others didn't.

We just took one another at his word and headed back to class, without even a hint of how much our lives were about to change.

# 5

## CAGED

### *Rameck*

OUR HANGOUT WAS behind the Clinton School. Whenever I went looking for my boys in Plainfield, I knew right
where to go. By the fall of 1989, I was sixteen years old and a
junior at University High. But every chance I got, I hung out
with my boys in Plainfield.

"Those boys ain't nothing but trouble," my aunt Nicole
often warned me. "You gonna get in a world of trouble following behind them."

Just four years apart, Nicole and I grew up as close as sister and brother. We played together at Ma's house and argued
all the time. She was super-protective of me. One time, an
older boy was bullying me just outside our house when Nicole
stuck her head out of the front door. He had me in a head-
lock, and she ran outside and beat him up. Sometimes,
though, it made me mad when she tried to pull rank and boss

me around, like trying to dictate who my friends were. What she didn't know was that the trouble had already begun. There were ten of us: Cast, Marley, Dre, Jamar, Buddy, Eric, Bookie, Sean, Shawn, and I. And we had earned quite the rep for beating people up.

My friends lived just around the corner from Ma, and most of us met in the first grade when we attended the Clinton School, a neighborhood elementary school for the children in our area. By the time we'd reached the seventh grade, they were already drinking beer. I'd take a sip, but at first I couldn't stand the taste of the stuff. We also began riding our bikes or taking the bus to neighboring towns and beating people up for no reason. Sometimes I couldn't go along. Neither Ma nor my mom tolerated my coming home whenever I pleased, so I couldn't make it if my boys were going to be out late. But I was with them one day when we planned to jump some boys who lived on another street.

My friends were having a beef with some guys from Arlington Avenue. My friends and I lived around Clinton Avenue, so it was a territorial thing. We planned to fight the other guys one day after school. I was going to University High School by then, but I skipped my classes and met my boys after school at Plainfield High.

"Rameck came through," one of my boys said when he saw me.

I felt so good that they were happy to see me.

We searched around the school for the other guys and waited, but we didn't see them. After a while, we left and headed toward the bus stop. When we got there, the Arlington

Street boys were in their cars waiting for us. A bunch of older guys, maybe their big brothers, were with them. They jumped out and surprised us. Everybody squared off with one person, and the older guys stood back and watched. One guy came at me and threw a punch. I ducked. I swung at him and popped him. He dropped to the ground, jumped up, and ran. My boys and I hopped onto a bus. They jumped into their cars and started following us.

At the next stop, some of their guys tried to board the bus. We begged the bus driver not to let them inside, but he kept saying he couldn't refuse a passenger. One of my friends rushed to the front to explain. When the driver opened the doors, a guy standing outside leaned into the bus and pulled out a fifty-dollar bill to pay for his fifteen or so buddies to board. But when the driver explained that he didn't have any change, the guy snatched my friend and tried to drag him off the bus. My friend grabbed onto a pole. That gave my boys and me enough time to run to the front, grab his legs, and pull him back. The driver took off.

We stayed on the bus until the end of the line. The other guys trailed in their cars. We begged the driver to keep going. He drove a couple more blocks. We had to try to make it to my friend's house just blocks away. It was do or die, so we took off running. About the same time, my friend's father heard a series of loud pops and rushed outside. He was staring at the bullet holes in his front porch when we made it there, out of breath.

Shawn and Marley had done time in juvenile detention. When they were thirteen, they beat up a white man and broke his nose. They served three years apiece for that, but when they got out, they went back to doing the same thing. A couple of my friends also were selling drugs.

Despite her problems, or perhaps because of them, my mother could see right through my friends. They were headed toward jail or death, she told me. She figured if she didn't intervene, I was headed that way, too. That's when she arranged for me to attend University High School. I told myself that she could make me go to high school in Newark, but she couldn't choose my friends. I was loyal. That was the code of the streets. These are your boys. You stick by them, and if necessary, you fight for them.

I knew my friends weren't innately bad or stupid. Sean and I were enrolled in the same advanced classes in junior high school. When we were little boys playing together in elementary school, we all had career dreams: fireman, police officer, basketball player, teacher. But the older we got, the less those dreams seemed real to us. The world around us seemed crazy: crack on every street corner, muggings, shootings.

In my friends, I saw myself: boys trying to become men with few good examples to follow. My father was a heroin addict who was in and out of jail. I didn't have anybody to emulate. I had uncles, but they were busy doing their own things. My uncle Rahman had moved out of Ma's house. Uncle Richard, who also had joined the Nation of Islam and changed his name to Rasheed, was developing a business that kept him busy. And Uncle Sheldon was away at college in Louisiana. They were all good guys, and I saw them regularly, but not as much as I saw my friends. I had no identity of my own, no sense of the kind of person I was or wanted to be. I was always looking for men to be like. I'd meet somebody who seemed pretty cool and tell myself I should try to be like him. When that wouldn't work out, I'd find somebody else. I just knew I wanted to be cool. My friends seemed cool, and for the moment, I was trying hard to be like them.

On a cold, clear Wednesday afternoon, the day before Thanksgiving in 1989, I was in Plainfield for the holiday break and, as usual, I was hanging out with six of my boys behind the school. We were just chilling, sitting on the steps at the back entrance of the school, talking and sharing forty-ounce bottles of Olde English malt liquor. A couple of the guys were smoking cigarettes.

A man we recognized as a crackhead approached our group and started begging one of my friends for some crack. The man, who appeared to be in his thirties, had once been a lifeguard at the community pool. His clothes were dirty, his hair matted and unkempt, his eyes glassy, red, and tired.

"I'll sell it to you, but you can't smoke it back here," my friend told him.

Our hangout was strictly a cool spot, not a place for selling or using drugs. That's where we drew the line. As strange as it may seem, we had our unwritten codes of honor. Kids sometimes wandered back there to play basketball on the concrete court, and we didn't want them exposed to that stuff. We figured we were protecting them, never mind that we were smoking, drinking, and throwing our own lives away.

My friend and the crackhead made a quick exchange, and the guy walked away.

A few minutes later, my friend looked up and saw the orange-and-blue glare of a crack pipe blazing from behind a big green Dumpster across the schoolyard.

"I told him not to do that shit back here," my friend said. "I ought to go beat his ass."

We set down our bottles on the steps and walked over to the Dumpster.

"What did I tell you? I told you not to be smoking back here," my friend yelled, chastising the man as though he were a child.

"I'm sorry, I'm sorry, I'm sorry," the man responded.

"Leave, now!"

"Hold on, I'm almost finished."

His lips were still wrapped around the crack pipe, and his eyes were closed when my friend punched him. The man dropped to his knees.

As liquor mixed with adrenaline and flowed through our bloodstreams, our judgment quickly warped. The atmosphere turned into a one-sided boxing match.

"Aw, man, you dropped him," somebody in the group shouted, laughing hysterically.

"You knocked him out," yelled another.

The crackhead stumbled back to his feet. Somebody else took a shot. The man hit the ground again. His pipe shattered into tiny pieces. He couldn't get up. This time, he moaned, rolled over, and began writhing in pain. By now, we were out of control, whooping it up, jumping from our ringside seats into the ring. Somebody else helped the man up, not out of mercy, but so all of us could participate in kicking his crack-smoking ass. I punched and kicked, too, thinking to myself he was probably somebody's father, in the back of an elementary school smoking crack when he should have been at home.

For twenty minutes, we punched and kicked him until he was red, black, and blue all over.

Suddenly, a daring thought popped into my head. I had bought a switchblade from my uncle Rasheed's small swap shop, and it happened to be in my coat pocket. I knew I would really impress my boys if I pulled it out now.

I whipped out my knife. For a couple of seconds I enjoyed the look of surprise and admiration in their eyes, the that-nigga-is-crazy look that can play on the ego of a confused teenaged boy and make him more dangerous than even he knew was possible.

"Un-huh, look what I got," I said, with a cold face, a puffed-out chest, an extended right arm, and the knife in a tight fist.

I felt a rush of fear. Lord knows I didn't want to stab this man. But I had pulled out the knife, and now my friends were looking at me, like, "What you gonna do?" If I did nothing, I would look like a punk.

I jabbed the crackhead lightly in the thigh right under his butt and quickly closed the blade, hoping I hadn't hurt him. There were more cheers. I tried to appear cool as I slipped the knife back in an inside coat pocket, but I was scared to death. Exhausted, we walked away and headed to the corner store.

Three of my friends left for the evening. The rest of us went back to the school to finish our beer. We walked along the side of the building to get back to our spot. When we reached the open court, we noticed a police car. Our first impulse was to run, but in a split second we decided to play it cool.

"Hey, come over here," one of the officers yelled to us, heading our way.

We stopped.

"We got a report that three guys who fit your description beat up this other guy pretty good," the officer said. "Were you back here?"

We figured he was fishing because there had been six of us.

"No, it wasn't us," we protested.

The officer started patting us down.

"He said one of you was wearing a black trench coat and had a knife," the officer continued.

My heart was sprinting, and my knees felt weak. I was wearing a black trench coat. The officer patted me down quickly. He missed the knife. I sighed deeply. The officer was about to let us go. Just then, his partner rushed over. Looking me dead in the eyes, he said to the other officer, "Did you search this one?"

"He searched me already," I said angrily. My heart picked up the pace again.

He ignored me and patted my pockets more carefully.

"I'd better not find a knife," the officer threatened. "If I find a knife, I'm gonna hurt you."

The officer reached into my inside pocket, pulled out some tissue and threw it to the ground. Next, he pulled out the knife.

"I told you not to lie to me," he said.

With a hand on each end of the wool scarf I had around

my neck, he began to choke me. He threw me against the police car and kneed me in the stomach.

Two other police cars and an ambulance carrying the injured man pulled up behind the school. One of the officers walked up to the ambulance and opened the door. The crackhead identified us.

The officers handcuffed us, pushed us into the car, and drove us to the precinct station. On the way, they kept telling us the man was in critical condition and might not make it. If they were trying to scare us, it worked. I had never been so afraid. I kept thinking, *"Oh my God, what if he dies?"*

At the precinct, we were charged with attempted murder. *Attempted murder!* We really hadn't been trying to kill the man. We just never thought about the consequences. I called my mother, but she was trying to teach me a lesson and didn't come to my rescue right away. In the meantime, two other officers transported us to a juvenile-detention center in Elizabeth. The officer driving the car joked with me about the knife.

"Man, that was a nice knife," he said. "I wish I'd caught you. I would've taken your knife and sent you about your business. Now, I gotta use this as evidence. That's a damn shame."

We had beaten up a crackhead. He didn't care.

My mother finally made it to the station, but I was already gone. She called a lawyer, but there was nothing he could do. It was a holiday weekend, and no judges were available. I had to stay locked up at least until Monday, four days away.

A security guard led me to my cell, a bare room hardly big enough for the two twin-sized cots that were side by side. A toilet sat on the concrete floor at the foot of the beds. Both beds were taken.

"Grab the floor," the security guard said, and threw me a blanket.

On Thanksgiving morning, I awakened early.

"Whew, I had this bad dream I got locked up," I mumbled, stretching and yawning.

I looked from one side of the room to the other. My Puerto Rican cellmates were still sleeping. I wasn't in my room at Ma's house. My nightmare was real.

Soon, the guards came to wake everybody else. They made us stand in line and escorted us to the cafeteria to eat horrible food. For one or two hours, we were allowed to watch television in a large room and play cards or go outside to a concrete courtyard to play basketball. Then it was back to the cell. My roommates spoke Spanish to one another, which made me uneasy. I figured they were plotting against me.

I spent most of my recreation time playing spades. I was good at spades, so one of the biggest guys in jail always chose me as his partner. The other guys figured we were friends and didn't mess with me. I was shocked at some of the stuff that went on there.

Late one night, I was lying on the floor unable to sleep when I heard a guy screaming in an adjacent cell. I lifted myself up but couldn't see past the cinderblock wall. I heard what sounded like underwear snapping. Terror swept through me like a cold chill. The guy next door was being raped.

Every afternoon, guys gathered around the tiny windows in their cells and talked to the girls headed home from school.

The girls assumed they would never see the guys again and talked real nasty to them. As I looked out the window and saw kids my age walking from school, going to McDonald's, laughing, and enjoying themselves, I suddenly felt sad. I wasn't free. I was locked in this nasty, disgusting place. I felt caged, like an animal. I had to eat when guards told me to eat, play when they told me to play, and use the toilet with everybody watching.

So many of the guys seemed resigned to this kind of life, as if it were their fate. I didn't get this sense from what they said. It was their mannerisms and the look in their eyes, a kind of cocky nonchalance that said that nothing much really mattered. To me, the experience was barbaric. "Never again," I told myself. I didn't want to spend my life this way.

The Monday after my arrest, I was released and placed on house arrest. The only place I could go was school. My probation officer visited regularly to make sure I was home. I saw Sam and George at school and made excuses for why we couldn't hang out. For a long time, I was too embarrassed to tell them the truth.

But my relationship with my boys in Plainfield was about to take a surprising turn. While we were all on house arrest, they began pressuring me to confess that I was the one who stabbed the crackhead. They were facing big time because of their previous records, and they were convinced that the stabbing—not the beating—had resulted in the attempted-murder charge. If I confessed to the stabbing, they said, they could get off on a lesser charge.

What about our loyalty to one another? I wondered. I

wasn't trying to get my friends into serious trouble, but my lawyer advised me to keep my mouth shut. "Just wait," he said, "anything could happen." The more I tried to explain to my friends why I hadn't confessed, the more impatient they became.

"I'm not going to jail for you," each of them warned.

In January, we attended a preliminary hearing before a judge. A couple of teachers and family members had written letters on my behalf, asking for mercy. The crackhead didn't show up. The judge set a new date. That date came, and the injured man missed that one, too. A third date was set. When he didn't show up for that one either, the judge threw out the charges. It was a highly unusual move on a charge as serious as attempted murder. Prosecutors still could have revived the case, but my lawyer pleaded with them to give me a break and not to pursue the matter. They didn't, and I got another chance.

I thanked God.

I felt as if I had been racing blindfolded to the edge of a cliff, just about to drop when the hand of God snatched me back to safety.

It wouldn't be the last time.

When I returned to University High after Thanksgiving break, I separated myself from my boys in Plainfield. I was ready to move on. I began spending more time with Sam and George.

# 6

# A BIG BREAK

*Sam*

THE MAN'S FACE looked familiar as he walked quickly toward my buddy Frank and me in the drizzling rain late one fall night in 1989. We were headed up Ludlow Street to the neighboring town of Elizabeth, a thirty-minute walk from the Dayton Street Projects.

This was one of many times when we were just walking the streets for fun. There wasn't much else to do. Our only attraction had been the Twin City Skating Rink, located on the border of Newark and Elizabeth. Dayton Street had been known for its skating rink, and what happened around the rink had helped earn the area its reputation. Some of the neighborhood thugs would hang out at the rink and plot against the teenagers from other neighborhoods who would come on Friday and Saturday nights to skate. They regularly attacked them on their way home and robbed them of their jewelry, money, and clothing. There were many nights when we saw a terrified teenager running through the adjacent park, trying to catch the Number 24 bus and escape the grip of the Dayton Street boys. Eventually, a few murders in the vicinity of the rink shut it down. That's how Newark was. You stayed on your side of town and all was fine.

Frank and I walked past Twin City on our way to Elizabeth. By then, it had been turned into a supermarket. Dried blood was still on the pavement.

The man with the familiar face caught up to us.

"Man, let me get two dollars," he said to Frank.

"I don't got it, man," Frank answered.

"Man, I know you got two dollars," he persisted. "Don't play with me."

"I don't got it," Frank repeated a bit louder.

The guy pulled open his oversized black goose-down jacket, lifted up his shirt, and pulled out a gun. He must have been desperate, because nobody pulled a gun on Frank. Frank had a rep around Dayton Street, and he hadn't gotten it by being a nice guy.

"What if I shoot you right now," the man threatened, his glassy eyes intense as he pointed the gun at Frank. "Would you give me two dollars then?"

"I don't got it, man," Frank said, still calm.

The guy turned to me, still pointing his gun at Frank.

"Marshall, I know you got it."

"I don't have it, man," I responded quickly. "I don't have it."

By now, he was frustrated and angry.

"Frank, I could shoot you right now," he said between clenched teeth.

Either Frank believed the guy didn't have the heart to shoot him, or he didn't care. With the man still pointing the gun at him, Frank turned his back and walked away. I followed on shaky legs and waited for bullets to slice through my back.

That was one of several times I came close to being a casualty of the madness all around me. I was sixteen, and my life was careening off-course with no direction. It had happened so quickly.

In my early teen years, kung fu lessons with Reggie had kept me away from the danger and temptations just beyond my door. I was working at McDonald's at the age of fifteen. Eager to get a job and help out at home, I'd altered my birth date by a year on the application to meet the minimum-age requirement. I wanted to do the right thing, but it seemed that everywhere I turned, someone or something was always pulling me in the opposite direction. By my junior year, I was drinking and hanging out late at night with older neighborhood boys eager to guide me into trouble.

It didn't take long for one of them to make a proposition I found it too difficult to turn down.

"Hey, Marshall, I got a way for you to make some money," he said.

He promised to split the profits of his crack sales with me if I invested money on the front end to help buy the drugs. The butterflies in my stomach told me this was wrong, but I told myself I needed the money. If I could take care of myself, Moms wouldn't have to worry about me. And why shouldn't I get a little piece of the action? Everybody around me was doing drugs on some level. The business certainly wouldn't dry up if I decided not to participate.

I didn't hustle on the streets, but I made a pickup once and helped bottle the tiny pellets into $10 vials. The first time I went on a pickup with my so-called business partner, we took the train to Harlem. When we walked up to the brownstone where we were to get the drugs, a guy was standing in the door wearing a gun in a holster. He patted us down. We walked into one room and turned over the money, then walked into another and picked up the drugs. It looked like the scene from a movie, with all the drugs piled on the table and guys standing around with guns, ready to shoot. We walked away with a plastic sack full of crack cocaine. As we stepped out of the house, I looked up and noticed the misty rain glistening in the street light. The night didn't even seem real.

"What in the hell did I get myself into?" I asked myself quietly.

I never went back. I made some quick cash, lots more than I was making at McDonald's, but no matter how I tried to justify it, I didn't feel good about what I was doing. After about a month, I told my friend that the benefits of the partnership just weren't worth the risks, and I eased my way out.

On January 19, 1990, the night of my seventeenth birthday, some of the fellows picked me up for drinks. We went to the Seth Boyden Projects, a set of low-rise projects separated from the Dayton Street development by an elementary school, to see a guy named Hock. He had just finished hustling when he got into the car with us. While sitting there in the parking lot, the other guys lit up some weed and started smoking.

"Yo, man, it's your birthday," Hock said. "I wanna wish you a happy birthday."

He handed my friend a package for me. It appeared to be cocaine.

"That's cool. Word up, word up," I responded.

I didn't want to seem ungrateful. One of the guys came up with an idea: we could make what was called a woolly, a drug-enhanced cigarette made by taking the tobacco out of a regular cigarette and mixing it with cocaine. One of my friends took two puffs and zonked out. His head bounced against the back of the car seat.

"Yo, man, it's your birthday," my other friend said. "We love you, man. You go."

Something on the inside said, "Don't do it." This was one of those times when I paid attention.

"Naw, man, that ain't me," I said.

"What, man? You think you better than that?" my friend said, offended.

"Naw, dog, I'm just too faded right now," I said, easing my way out of trouble again. "Plus I gotta go to work tomorrow."

They backed off. But I still had a difficult time saying no to my friends, even when I knew they were wrong. I wasn't afraid of them; I was afraid of what they would think of me. I didn't want to appear weak or afraid. That could have made me a constant target in my neighborhood. It was easier to just go along. And I admit, sometimes the adrenaline rush of getting away with something wrong felt good. I lived for the moment, too afraid to imagine a future that could be cut short any day.

I was kicking it on the corner with four of my boys one day in the summer between my junior and senior years when one of them came up with a moneymaking scheme: we could rob drug dealers. At seventeen, I was one of the younger ones. Another guy in the group was fifteen, and the other two were in their twenties. The suggestion took hold quickly as my friends added their individual touches. We would all dress in black. We would ride around Newark and neighboring cities in which there were hot drug markets, target young, inexperienced dealers, jump out on them with a gun, take their money, and split it four ways.

At first it seemed like a fantasy. But the more we talked, the more real it became. We thought we were justified since we were just targeting drug dealers.

The butterflies in my stomach started acting up again, but I played it cool and nodded in agreement.

The first couple of times, the operation went smoothly. I drove and sat in the car while they did their thing. I got my cut, and it didn't seem like a big deal.

But one evening as I was walking home from a Kentucky Fried Chicken after an exhausting game of basketball, one of the guys approached me.

"Man, why don't you drive out tonight?" he suggested.

I had bought a car during the school year a few months earlier, and the guys were ready to score again.

"Aw, man, I don't feel like it," I said, the butterflies in my stomach fluttering like crazy.

"Come on, Marshall," my friend pleaded.

I gave in. The two of us walked back to my house to get my car, picked up the other two guys, and headed out. We rode around for a while until we spotted about ten to twelve teenagers hanging out on a hot drug corner in Montclair. We figured they were dealers.

"Let's get them right there," one of the guys said from the back seat.

I stopped the car and my friends jumped out on the crowd. This time, I joined them. My friend pulled out his gun and shouted, "Empty your pockets!"

The other three of us began patting down pockets, pulling out wads of cash. All of a sudden, another car, a brown, four-door Citation, rolled up. The driver and front-seat passenger were young guys, probably in their twenties. The four of us didn't recognize them. The guys we were robbing didn't react like they knew them, either.

"What in the hell is going on?" I whispered.

I was close enough to peer into the car, and my eyes quickly fell upon what appeared to be a police radio mounted to the floor.

I began backing away.

"21 Jump! 21 Jump!" I shouted, trying to alert my friends that a police officer was on the scene. (At the time, *21 Jump Street,* a television series featuring young undercover cops, was popular.)

I was about twenty feet away when police cars began whizzing toward the scene from every direction. I kept walking, cool at first, as though I was just a passerby. But as I rounded the corner out of sight, I took off running. When I was far enough away, I stopped and rested my hands on my knees to catch my breath. Sweat rolled, like tears, from every corner of my face. My stomach did somersaults. I waited there a few minutes and calmed myself down, then doubled back to the scene to pick up my car. It was gone. My friends were gone. The police and the crowd of dealers were gone.

I hailed a taxi to take me home. But I slept little that night, worrying about what would happen next.

I figured my car had been towed, and I called the town's towing company the next morning. An employee told me that my car was on hold and that I needed to call the Montclair Police Department. My throat was so dry I could hardly swallow as I punched in the numbers to the police department. An officer told me to come to the precinct house to answer some questions. All three of my friends had been arrested.

I confided in my sister Fellease, who drove me to the police station. She assured me that the police would release me in her custody since I was a juvenile. And I was sure that my friends, most of whom had already spent time in juvenile detention, would see my arrest as a medal of badness, something to be respected.

"Are you Marshall?" one of the officers asked as I entered.

I thought it strange that he knew my middle name, which was used only by my family and friends. The officer escorted me to a small, spare room with a desk and two chairs. He sat on one side of the desk, and I sat on the other. He clicked on a tape recorder.

"Someone said you were involved in an incident last night in Montclair," the officer said.

"What incident was that?" I asked, trying to appear clueless.

The officer described the robbery. I could have lied and told him that my friends had put a gun to my head and made me drive. Or, I could have said they had stolen my car. But I would have to live with the results of the lie. I came clean. He arrested me, charged me with armed robbery, and sent me to a juvenile-detention center in Newark. A judge refused to release me in my sister's custody because a gun had been involved.

The detention center was divided into four units based on the type of crime committed. I landed in Unit 1, where juveniles arrested for violent crimes were assigned.

I was led to a small room with a metal cot screwed to the middle of the floor and no outside windows. I was handed a sheet to use as a cover. I felt ashamed. Day and night I sat there thinking, "How could I disappoint Moms like this? All she asked of me was to get an education. How could I be dumb enough to participate in a robbery? How could I end up here? I'm a better person than this. Aren't I?"

I was seventeen. What would happen to me now?

Every day, I sat on my cot and thought: If given another chance, how could I change my life? I wondered what George and Rameck were doing with their summer. I had no idea Rameck had already experienced what I was going through.

Even behind bars, it was hard to stay out of trouble. Brothers were always picking fights. I was outside playing basketball one day and walked over to a table to get something to drink. As I reached for a paper cup and the water pitcher, one of the tough guys snatched the pitcher.

"That's mine," he said, staring me down, clearly trying to mark his territory.

"This is everybody's water," I retorted. "What you mean, it's yours?"

One of his partners quickly piped in: "Naw, man, that's Marshall, he's cool."

A potential blowup had been deflated. I didn't want to get into a fight and make my troubles worse.

The word on the street was that prosecutors were considering trying me as an adult, which could result in a jail sentence of three to ten years. The thought of spending ten years in jail petrified me. My parents had been visiting every other day, and they hired an attorney. Within a few weeks, he worked out a plea bargain. I would serve 365 days in juvenile detention in exchange for a guilty plea.

On the day I was scheduled to go to court to accept the plea agreement, my attorney rushed back to my holding cell with another offer: a two-year suspended sentence and two years of probation for my guilty plea. I was reluctant to accept it until my lawyer explained that I wouldn't have to serve the suspended sentence as long as I stayed out of trouble and abided by the terms of my probation. Since I was a juvenile, the crime would not appear on my permanent record.

I'll never forget that court hearing. I had to face a judge, plead guilty, and accept the sentence agreed to in the plea bargain. My lawyer had not had a chance to explain the new agreement to my family, who were waiting in the audience. Moms was sitting behind me in the front row, separated from me by a wooden partition. When the judge announced my sentence, she mistakenly thought he was sentencing me to serve two years in jail.

"Your Honor, just take me," she cried out. "He's a young boy. He didn't know what he was doing. Please, take me!"

I was disgusted with myself. But I had just gotten the biggest break of my life. I told myself I would never end up behind bars again. Somehow, I would change my life.

I walked away from court that day after spending four weeks in juvenile detention.

Summer was ending, and I was about to enter my senior year. I had never been so determined to succeed. There'd been times when I hadn't taken the pact I made with George and Rameck seriously, but I certainly did now. I could have gone to prison for ten years. Suddenly, spending eight years in college didn't seem like a bad idea.

I remembered that a couple of times George had mentioned wanting to become a dentist. It amazed me that he could dream so big. I had thought about pursuing a career as a big-time business tycoon, but that dream had faded as I grew older. It seemed easier to me to give up my ambitions than to have to face the disappointment of not fulfilling them. I often asked George how he managed to stay focused on his dream.

"I just believe it can happen," he would say to me.

I used to wonder what George had in his life that I didn't. I realized that he believed in himself and believed something mystical would happen for him. Many times it did. For one reason or another, George had luck that way. Things appeared to work in his favor. I felt it was God's way of rewarding him for remaining so focused. I always admired his patient virtue and never-say-die attitude.

I didn't tell Rameck and George about my arrest—at least not right away. I wasn't sure what they would think of me if they knew. Instead, I shifted my focus to getting into college.

I wanted to share the news about my college plans with my boys from the neighborhood. One of the older guys who had participated in the armed robbery was out of jail, awaiting his trial. We were hanging out on the stoop near the basketball court at Dayton Street Elementary with two other guys when I brought up the subject.

"Man, I'm thinking about going on to college," I said.

They burst out laughing.

"What? College? Man, that ain't gon' never happen," my friend said.

I sat quietly and took their taunts. I didn't blame them for being unable to visualize my going to college. I could hardly see it myself. I just knew that I wanted more out of my life, even if I couldn't quite define what more I wanted. I knew, too, that I had to let these guys go. I would never be able to rise with them tugging at my heels.

That was the last day I hung with them.

Eventually, the three others involved all got jail time. They had previous records, and each of the cases was handled separately. The fifteen-year-old, the youngest of the four of us, was sentenced to three years for the crime. One of the older guys, the one who had pulled the gun, got seven years; the other one, five.

Years later, I would encounter my old friends again. And I would be jolted by the reality of what my life could have become.

# 7

## HOPE

### *George*

AND THEN BEFORE WE KNEW IT, we were seniors.

"How you coming along with that application, man?" I asked Sam and Rameck almost daily once the school year began. I wanted to make sure they kept up their end of the deal.

By January, most of our classmates were either still working on their college applications or waiting for a response. A few of the early birds had already received acceptance letters.

Rameck still planned to apply to Howard University, and despite his promise Sam couldn't decide whether he wanted to spend eight years in medical school or pursue a degree in business. I halfheartedly applied to two other colleges, but my focus was on the Pre-Medical/Pre-Dental Plus Program at Seton Hall. As the deadline drew near, our competitiveness helped us rush the process along. When one of us finished part of the application and bragged about it, the other two hurried to complete theirs.

By early spring we were invited to Seton Hall for an interview. I went first. My mother drove me to South Orange, a suburb about a half-hour from downtown Newark. We knew immediately when we crossed the border. On one side, houses were boarded up, the streets were full of litter, and people were hanging on the corner in the middle of the day. On the other, houses and lawns were magazine-cover beautiful, the streets were clean, and the air was quiet.

For the entire ride, I kept wondering whether I could really make it in college. I thought I'd have to be a genius to get in, and I was scared to death. My mother and I found our way to the campus, past the old buildings and perfectly primped lawn, to the basement office of Carla Dickson, the student development specialist for the program. Her smile seemed genuine as she greeted us. My heart started racing like Carl Lewis when she began the questions.

She asked why I wanted to become a doctor. I tried to look calm as I shared with her the story of the dentist who had first sparked my interest in dentistry. She asked questions about my family and background. When she asked where I wanted to work after graduation, I figured she was trying to gauge whether I would be interested in returning to work in a community like the one where I grew up. My dream has always been to open a dental clinic in Newark someday, and that's what I told her. Later I discovered that I had been right: one of the goals of the Pre-Medical/Pre-Dental Plus Program is to train medical professionals to staff hospitals and clinics in urban areas.

Carla met Rameck and Sam in later interviews. I had told her they were my friends and that we wanted to go to college together. When it was Sam's turn to be interviewed, ever the analyst, he showed up with a list of questions: Would he have to change to fit in at Seton Hall? How would he be able to afford it? What kind of support could he expect from the university?

It was important to all three of us that, no matter where we went to college, we didn't forget where we came from or change our hip-hop style. Carla tried to reassure Sam that he wouldn't have to change to succeed at Seton Hall and that, if accepted, he would receive financial aid and counseling from the university. The reassuring tone of the interviews gave us all confidence that we would be accepted.

A few weeks later, I returned home from school and found a letter to me from Seton Hall on the table. I had been accepted to the program. I called Sam and Rameck. They, too, had received acceptance letters.

In the meantime, Rameck had also been accepted to Howard University. The university had even assigned him a room. But when he received a letter asking for a deposit to secure the room, he couldn't come up with the money before the deadline, and it occurred to him that he would not be able to afford Howard without financial aid. Finally, Rameck and Sam decided that the program at Seton Hall was too good to pass up. We didn't say anything more to solidify our pact, but from then on our commitment to one another became stronger. We began to plan our future together.

For me, getting accepted into Seton Hall relieved the pressure of not knowing for sure what would happen next. I could finally relax and enjoy my senior year.

In our final days of school, Rameck, Sam, and I did the kinds of things that seniors everywhere do to make memories of their last year.

I took my girlfriend to the prom. Sam and Rameck brought dates, too. Shahid and I put our money together, rented a limousine, and double-dated. The cost of the limo and tuxedo hit my pockets pretty hard, and I didn't enjoy myself. I didn't even dance.

My girlfriend and I had been dating for about seven months. I really liked her, and I was a faithful kind of guy. But I was about to embark on the greatest challenge of my life, and I didn't want any distractions. About a month later, we broke up.

Breaking up with my girlfriend whenever I started a new phase of my life would become a pattern.

And finally, there was graduation.

It was one of few times that I saw my father, who joined the rest of my family in the auditorium at University High. Sam's and Rameck's families were there, too. They snapped photos and cheered as we marched into the auditorium in our burgundy caps and gowns. The day was a scorcher, at least ninety degrees, and some of the guys rebelled by wearing shorts, instead of the traditional dress slacks, under their gowns. The three of us played by the rules and wore the traditional attire.

For our parents, this was a historic event. Their sons were not only headed to college, but were planning to become doctors. We had survived the streets of Newark, and that was no small reason to be grateful. Boys our age were dying every day.

Our friend Ahi Baraka had barely survived the year before. A man who had robbed Ahi's older brother of $3 spotted the brothers riding through the neighborhood about one A.M. the next morning and fired into their car. Ahi, sitting in the passenger seat, ducked when he heard gunshots but was wounded in the head.

Amazingly, Ahi recovered and made it back to school in time to graduate with the rest of us.

I don't remember much of the pomp and circumstance of our graduation day. But I remember the emotion of it. We all knew our lives were about to change big-time. We all had dreams, but who really knew whether those dreams would materialize? Until that moment, our paths had been set. Elementary school. Junior high. High school.

Now we were on our own.

As I sat in the auditorium as a student at University High for the last moments, I was sad about leaving my classmates. But I also felt calm.

I knew I wouldn't have to face the uncertainty of the future alone.

# George on
# PEER PRESSURE

People often ask me how I avoided getting caught up in some of the negative things that many of the guys in my neighborhood were doing when I was growing up. I've often thought about that question myself. There wasn't anything special about me. But I'd have to say that the kinds of friends I chose—positive guys who wanted to do the right thing—made a huge difference in how my life turned out.

In my experience, friends have more influence on one another's lives than almost anyone else does, especially in those teenage years when kids are trying to discover who they really are. So hooking up with the wrong crowd can really drag you down.

Think about it. Most kids, rich or poor, spend more time with their friends than with their parents. They're together all day at school. They're together in the neighborhood after school. And they're together on the weekends. Maybe they even spend their summers together at summer camp. Their friends define what is acceptable and cool. I've never known a kid who doesn't want to be accepted, myself included. That can be particularly dangerous among boys because something about our makeup or upbringing suggests that to be macho is to be cool. And the wrong set of friends can persuade us that to prove how tough we are, we have to do crazy things, from small acts of defiance or bravado—like shoplifting, daring kids to do things we'd never do ourselves, or bullying—to more serious behavior, like using or selling drugs, getting into fights, stealing cars, robbing people, or worse. That's why it's so important to hang with the right people.

As a kid, I aligned myself with guys who thought like me; guys who did their work in school and avoided the negative stuff. And many of the friends I chose in my neighborhood were younger. I guess in some ways that satisfied my need to be accepted, because they looked up to me. I was pretty much winging it back then, just doing what felt right to me. But with hindsight, I realize that avoiding the older, more intimidating boys, and even becoming a big brother to my friends, was an excellent strategy. It allowed me to set the standard in my group for what was cool. I wasn't into drug dealing, stealing, or scheming, so my friends weren't, either. There were always other guys doing other things, but they didn't bother me, and I didn't bother them.

In high school, I followed the same pattern and chose friends who did well in school but still liked to have fun. That's what drew me to Rameck and Sam. We had the same core desire to make something of our lives, and we brought out the best in one another. We weren't exactly alike, but that was okay. They never tried to pressure me to indulge. In fact, they never even drank in front of me, so we were cool. I had to put up with some good-natured ribbing every now and then from some of our friends, but I knew it was all in fun. I suppose those were the times when my own confidence came into play. I didn't like the taste of alcohol, and that was that.

Even though Rameck and Sam would eventually follow neighborhood friends into trouble, I admire them for also having the good sense to recognize that those friends were no good for them, and for having the guts to break away.

I'm not foolish enough to believe that I was able to avoid negative peer pressure alone. In the kind of neighborhood where I grew up, it would have been easy to believe that what I saw was all there was to life. But I had a third-grade teacher who taught me how to dream and to think for myself. I had a friend whose father spent good time with me and made me feel I was worthy of a father's love. And most of all, I had a mother who worked hard and managed to keep things straight at home.

When I look back over my life and the lives of my friends, I also see that involvement in school and community activities helped us to avoid the negative pull of our peers. I joined the Shakespeare Club in elementary school and the Police Athletic League in elementary and junior high, and I played baseball in high school. Sam took karate lessons from grade school through his early years in high school and also played on our high-school baseball team. And Rameck took drama lessons in junior high school, and in high school he joined the drama club and helped start the United Students Organization. Those activities gave us fun things with which to occupy our minds and our time. But perhaps even more valuable, they provided safe places for us to meet other kids who shared the same interests.

It's hard to have the confidence, especially in the teen years, to stand up for what you believe is right when people all around you are pulled in another direction. That's where having positive friendships can really help. If you find the right guys to hang with—guys you trust, who share your values and your friendship—you'll find that you can stand up to almost anything.

You may even be surprised how much you can accomplish together. I certainly was.

# 8

# SUMMER ODYSSEY

## *Rameck*

I WAS AS EXCITED as a kid going away to summer camp for the first time when Sam, George, and I left home for Seton Hall in June before our freshman year.

We were among the ten students accepted into the Pre-Medical/Pre-Dental Plus program that year. All of us had been recruited from urban New Jersey high schools, and we had to spend six weeks of the summer on campus to get some remediation. The goal was to bring us up to par academically with students who would be sitting next to us in class in the fall.

For the first time in years, life would be stable for me, with no more moving from one relative's house to another. And that felt good. I was finally over my disappointment that I wouldn't be able to attend Howard University with Ahi and Hasaan. Ahi was a student activist at University High, respected by students and teachers. And he was also one of my closest friends.

My uncles, who belonged to the Nation of Islam, and Bill, the barbershop owner, had taught me that I had a responsibility to help my community. Ahi believed that, too. We had the same ideas. That's what had attracted me to him.

The two of us had grown even closer when we helped plan the student protest against the Board of Education. Ahi and I would sit in his room and talk, like young intellectuals, about the condition of our people. We were pissed that the school system didn't offer a single class in African-American or Hispanic history, though African-American and Hispanic students made up the bulk of the population in the schools.

On the day of the protest, we felt like civil-rights activists, fighting for something we truly believed in. Some school officials and other detractors suspected that Ahi's father had put us up to it. But they were wrong.

I knew Mr. Baraka was a poet. Sometimes when I was at his house, he would have functions in the basement, a meeting on some issue or a party with friends reciting poetry to the beat of jazz music. But I didn't realize until much later that he was one of the nation's most prominent black intellectuals.

Ahi never mentioned it. I should have figured it out by the way people responded to him. "That's Amiri Baraka's son," they would say.

I saw Amiri Baraka as my friend's father, who, unlike so many other of my friends' fathers, was at home with his family, there to give his sons guidance, advice, and, of course, money. It was Mr. Baraka who paid for the limousine when Ahi, Hasaan, and I triple-dated for the prom.

A child quite naturally is influenced by a parent's philosophies and beliefs, but Mr. Baraka never preached to us or interjected himself into our business. He let us find our own way.

When I heard that Ahi had been shot at the end of our junior year in high school, I had never been so scared. I hadn't heard anything when I showed up at school that morning, but I noticed an unusual crowd of teachers and students standing outside the school. Some of them were crying.

"What's going on?" I asked the first person I saw.

When they told me, all I could do was run. I didn't know whether he was alive or dead. My heart beat faster than it ever had. Hasaan and some of Ahi's other good friends were already standing outside the Baraka home, waiting to hear if he was okay.

Ahi survived, and he would attend Howard University in the fall, when I would begin my freshman year at Seton Hall.

On campus that summer, I was excited to have my own twin bed, a telephone, and a desk. Each room had central air and heat, carpeting, and a bathroom shared with two other suitemates.

Sam and I were roommates, and George shared the same suite with another guy. I tacked oversized posters of rappers to the wall on my side of the room and set up my radio and a small refrigerator that I had bought from my uncle's swap shop. We kept the radio tuned to a station that woke us each morning to the same song: "As long as you keep your head to the sky, be optimistic. . . ."

Sam said it motivated him.

I needed some inspiration, because my fantasy of a fun-filled summer camp met reality the first week. The program was more like boot camp, requiring more discipline, hard work, and effort than I had ever given anything before.

We rose each day by seven A.M. for breakfast and then headed to the lecture halls for eight A.M. classes. Assessment tests determined the levels of math we took. Sam and I tested into pre-calculus, and George took intermediate algebra. He knew he was just as smart as the two of us, so he would enroll in summer school the following year to catch up. We also took chemistry, chemistry lab, computer skills, and critical-thinking courses that summer.

We were among the 110 EOP students attending summer school that year. The ten students in our group got to mingle with the other students during lunch and dinner and in a couple of large classes, like English. Sam, George, and I walked to class together and usually sat right next to one another. Most of the classes were small, no more than the ten people in the Pre-Medical/Pre-Dental Plus program. The professors pushed me to use my brain, which had been in the snooze mode practically all four years of high school. I couldn't get away with cheating or just skipping homework. I was learning something new every day and found I was eager to learn more. I realized I didn't mind school, as long as I wasn't bored.

We studied together in the evenings and compared grades,

and we each competed to do as well as the others. When one of us made an A on a test, the other two were like, "Yo, man, I'm gonna get me an A, too." The three of us managed to keep up with our peers and, eventually, outperform them. When classes ended each day at five P.M., all of the students in the program had to attend a one-hour tutoring session. A team of four tutors, one for each subject, milled around the room and worked with us in the areas where we needed help. The tutors were a mix of professors and upperclassmen, and they covered basic lessons the three of us had missed in high school. I loved those sessions. Those guys made even calculus seem simple. Our test scores began rising from the 70s to the 90s.

Our group would take a short dinner break at six P.M., then head for our rooms to study until nine P.M. We weren't allowed to watch television while we were studying, and we had to keep the doors to our dorm rooms open while our counselors, Maria, Ron, and Tawana, walked the halls to make sure we weren't goofing off. We even had a mandatory bedtime: ten P.M. The counselors visited our rooms to make sure the lights were out.

They were treating us like babies, and I couldn't stand it. In time, I would lead a mini-rebellion.

But Sam and I often stayed up talking long after the lights went out, sometimes until two or three o'clock the next morning, a ritual that would continue throughout college and medical school. We spent much of the time just reflecting on how our lives were changing. We also used that time to settle our differences.

"Man, you really pissed me off today," one of us would say.

Then the conversation would bounce from one side of the room to the other in the dark until we were both satisfied that the issue had been resolved. After that, we were cool again, and I was ready to move the conversation on to more serious stuff, like girls.

Unlike in high school, Sam, George, and I attended every class, did all of the assigned homework, studied together, and made good grades in every subject. I was determined to prove to myself that I belonged here. But I couldn't look too far ahead. I had trouble believing I would actually become a doctor someday.

Carla Dickson, the counselor who had interviewed us and recommended us for the program, seemed to know intuitively that many of her students felt that way. She offered encouragement the first day of class.

"You are doctors," she told us in her opening remarks. "You guys have to visualize yourselves as doctors."

It was not the first time Carla would anticipate what we were feeling and say just the right thing to boost our confidence. She taught a course called "Becoming a Master Student," which focused on basic survival skills: how to take notes effectively, study for tests, manage our time, dress for a job interview, and control our temperament. The assignments she gave all had purpose. In class one day, she instructed each of us to pretend we were getting a big award at a banquet—any award we wanted—and had been asked to give an acceptance speech. Our assignment was to write the speech and read it in front of the entire class. The exercise was designed not just to work on our writing skills, but to help build our confidence enough so that we would feel at ease speaking before a room full of strangers. Subtly, she was working on our self-esteem.

Carla also gave us good practical advice to attract our professors' attention and show them we were serious: get to class on time, sit in the first two rows, and participate in class discussions. She even conducted role-playing exercises to help us learn how to negotiate with teachers and administrators to resolve potential problems. Carla arrived on campus early and stayed late every day. Sam, George, and I bonded with her right away.

As part of the program, the students occasionally attended health and diversity workshops that gave us a chance to meet and spend time with African-American doctors.

One weekend, we rode a bus to a farm in Pottstown, Pennsylvania, for a retreat. Most of us had never spent any time in the country, so we looked forward to the trip. The farm was spread over several acres, but it was set up for large group visits. Each cabin was equipped with bunk beds. The girls stayed together in one cabin and the guys in another. Breakfast in the dining room of the main house was awesome—homemade biscuits, grits, fresh eggs, and bacon.

During the day we met in a large community room for seminars on a wide range of subjects, such as drugs and AIDS education, exercise, and nutrition. For recreation, we played basketball and swam. One night, we walked along a trail through the woods, stopped at a camp, roasted marshmallows, and told stories and silly jokes around a fire. There, the black-ness of night was peaceful: no sirens, no gunshots, no need to constantly look over our shoulders.

The requirements of the summer program consumed every minute of our day, and we were not the least bit happy about that, especially in sunny, 90-degree weather when we ached to get outside and shoot some hoops. I complained endlessly. I had never studied so hard before, and I was unaccustomed to being monitored so closely and having so little free time. Soon, other students were complaining, too. As the program drew to a close, we concocted a plan to air our dissatisfaction.

Carla had asked us to create a bulletin board about the Pre-Medical/Pre-Dental Plus Program in the hallway outside her basement office. The bulletin-board project had become a sort of closing tradition. Each year, students tried to be cre-ative in expressing their views of the program. When the ten of us met to discuss the project, we decided to depict our-selves as mental prisoners. We would draw pictures of stu-dents dressed in prison garb, standing behind prison bars under the name of the program. We excitedly planned the details of how to execute our little masterpiece.

But somehow Carla found out about our plans.

We were all in our dorm rooms late one afternoon when we heard her voice over the intercom summoning the stu-dents and counselors to the lounge area outside the third floor. She had never done this before, so we knew something was wrong. When we'd assembled, I took one look at Carla's face and knew we were in trouble.

"So, you think you're in prison, huh?" she asked rhetorically. We were busted.

"This is nothing like prison," she continued. "Your future is going to be brighter than bright. You just don't see it now. Because of this program, you're going to be able to make it through college with no problems. I know it's hard, but realize that you have an opportunity to make a difference in your lives."

She was looking at our faces as she spoke, but I had trouble holding my head up to make eye contact with her. It had never occurred to me that what we'd done would hurt her so much. She was angry, yes, but she was even more deeply hurt. Because she gave so much of herself to the program, she was personally offended by our plans. I had never seen her this way.

"The nerve of you guys," Carla fumed, "depicting this program by showing yourselves behind bars. Over my dead body!"

She stormed out, leaving us alone in an uncomfortable silence. Someone in the group had snitched, but we were too ashamed even to waste time trying to figure out who had done it. We just slunk back to our rooms.

Later, we decided on a simpler project. We hung a picture and brief biography of each of ourselves on the bulletin board.

Our class ultimately would become one of the program's most successful. Seven of us would complete college and medical school and become doctors, and another student would earn a medical degree, as well as a master's in public health from Johns Hopkins University. Only two students would drop out of Seton Hall and transfer to other schools.

Sam, George, and I completed the summer program with A's and B's in all of our classes.

The program closed with a banquet the night before our final exam. I was one of two students who received a book scholarship for outstanding academic performance. A state senator presented the award.

Our keynote speaker, Dr. Francis Blackman, a pulmonary specialist who was president of the North Jersey Medical Society, emphasized the continued need for the Pre-Medical/ Pre-Dental Plus Program. He said that the nation's health-care system is still a dual system in which African Americans, especially the poor, receive inferior treatment. As a result, he said, the health outlook for African Americans is worse, and our life span is still far shorter than that of white Americans.

My complaints about the program seemed to melt away at the banquet. Our parents were there, as well as all of the professors and counselors who had helped with the program. Everybody was celebrating us for doing well, something that was new for me. The banquet was like a pep rally before the big game. It left us motivated to face the next four years.

# 9
---

# EARTH ANGEL

## *Sam*

IT WAS THE FALL OF 1990, and Carla Dickson was attending the Black Issues Conference in New Brunswick when she heard an author who would change her life—and ours.

Jawanza Kunjufu, an education consultant, was discussing his series of books, *The Conspiracy to Destroy Black Boys.* He described how smart, energetic, and hopeful black boys enter school systems so inadequately prepared to educate them that the boys begin to lose interest as early as the fourth grade and are often lost to the streets by high school. He proposed mentoring as a solution and asked the men in the audience to stand. He admonished them to go back to their communities and become mentors to the black boys who needed them.

Carla was so moved by the workshop that when he'd finished talking she headed for the booth where he was signing his books. The crowd was so thick that, at no more than five feet tall, she couldn't even hope to catch a glimpse of him. So she waited at the end of the line and prayed that his books wouldn't sell out before she made it to the table.

As Carla tells it, she lost track of time while replaying Kunjufu's words in her mind. When she finally made it to the front of the line, she bought a set of books and shook the author's hand. He wrote down her name and asked her to return to the table later to pick up the books. To fill the time, she wandered around the Ramada Hotel and faked interest in other exhibits for about forty-five minutes. She returned to Kunjufu's table, but he still had not signed her books. She attended another workshop, and by the end she was so tired that she nearly forgot to retrieve the books. People rushed by her as she walked slowly past all of the booths. Suddenly, she heard a man's voice behind her.

"Here are your books," he said.

It was Kunjufu. In her hotel room, she flipped open the cover of the first book and read the inscription:

"Carla, go out and save our black boys," it said.

The following spring, George, Rameck, and I showed up in her office for an interview.

She says that when she met George, she could tell that he really wanted to be a dentist and that Rameck and I were more skeptical. She could see that Rameck wanted to trust her and wanted to come to Seton Hall, though he didn't really know why. She knew right away that I carried a lot of weight, and she declares I took over, interviewing her.

But Carla says she liked us right away and immediately saw us as a unit. She feared that if one of us dropped out of the program, she risked losing all three of us. She vowed not to allow that to happen, and she became our angel, guiding, protecting, and pushing us as we traveled blindly from the comforts and dangers of our old world through the challenging new ones at Seton Hall.

Carla planned every detail of student life in the Pre-Medical/Pre-Dental Plus program, right down to who would be roommates with whom. Her job was to figure out the weaknesses of the students in the program—whether those weaknesses were academic, social, environmental, or personal—and find a way to help us strengthen them. Her first move was to assign Rameck and me as roommates for the summer program, and to place George in the same suite but with another roommate across the hall. She says she didn't want our reservations to influence George. She figured if she could keep George excited, he would work on us.

Several times over the years at Seton Hall, I received a grade less than I thought I deserved in a class and complained to Carla. She wouldn't allow me to get by with just complaining. She persuaded me to make an appointment to talk to the professor to try to understand why I had received the lower mark and to make my case for myself. More times than not, her advice worked.

Soon I began hanging out in her office during my spare time. I loved talking to her. She would sit behind her desk and sometimes not utter a word. She would look at me and listen. Other times, though, she did most of the talking. But when she talked to me, she rarely judged, or preached, or gave an automatic list of steps to follow. She asked questions: "Well, what do you think you should do about that?" "What is your gut telling you to do?" She helped guide me to an answer that was already inside me.

Carla didn't try to change us, and that was important. Rameck, George, and I wanted to be able to enjoy college without suddenly looking or sounding like boys who went to prep schools all of their lives. We liked our 'hood gear: baggy jeans, boots, and rap music. Still do. Carla accepted that. She always seemed to know how to reach us and just what to say. Of the three of us, I grew closest to her, perhaps because I was the most needy emotionally.

But Carla could be tough, and she wasn't the least bit intimidated by three teenage boys who sometimes resented being pushed so hard. She would plant her tiny frame in front of one of us, stand toe-to-toe, and tell us to our faces when she thought we were being selfish, lazy, or just plain dumb. And guess what? We listened. She always came across as real, not like a snooty professor with a bunch of fake, impractical wisdom. More like a big sister, passing on life lessons learned firsthand. The door to her office was always open, and she gave us her home telephone number.

After my first couple of years of college, I grew tired of the countless hours of studying and never quite feeling like I belonged, even with Rameck and George constantly at my side. One night, when I felt especially dejected, I called Carla at home and began to vent my frustration.

As usual, she listened while I contemplated whether to drop out of college. Then, she asked:

"Sam, what do you have to return to?"

That stopped my spiral into self-pity because the truth was, if I left college I had nothing but trouble waiting at home.

"This is about more than you," she continued. "There are kids behind the gates in your neighborhood, wanting to be doctors. They need you to do well for this program to continue to get funded. You have to pave the way for them."

Carla had grown up in East Orange, two blocks from Newark, with a mother who was a teacher and a father who was a Tuskegee airman. She was the youngest of three girls—her sisters are a teacher and a pediatrician—and was especially close to her father. She attended public schools. As an adult, she once attended a workshop that focused on the longtime disparities between suburban schools and those in the inner city. Carla was shocked and furious to learn, for example, that the science lab at her alma mater in East Orange contained burners that were obsolete and had not worked ten years before she'd even arrived at the school. Meanwhile, schools in the suburbs had all the latest equipment.

In the neighborhood where she was raised, poor, working- and middle-class black families all lived on the same block. Neighbors knew one another and helped one another out. Poor children growing up in homes without daddies got to talk regularly to the hardworking men in the community: the black pilot, construction worker, or teacher who lived across the street or down the block. It saddened Carla that her generation of black professionals fled the neighborhoods of their youth for the suburbs, leaving behind such poverty and hopelessness. She often talked to us about the need for more black professionals to stay and fight for the inner city. And to this day, Rameck and I still live in neighborhoods like the ones where we were raised, and George lives in the same apartment where he grew up, a block from where the old Stella Wright Projects once stood. They were demolished recently and replaced with low-income town houses as part of an inner-city revitalization project.

Many of the practical lessons that Carla brings to her survival-skills class stem from her own experience as one of the few black students at Drexel University in 1975. She ultimately transferred to Seton Hall, closer to home, and earned a bachelor's degree in business management.

I rarely talked to anyone about my family. Some things I never even told George or Rameck. They had their own burdens. Whenever a family matter bothered me, I just shoved it into my inner "box." But when I hung out in Carla's office, she asked questions about my family. I was reluctant to talk at first, afraid of what would happen if I let her see all the ugliness in my box. But she seemed genuinely interested in me. She talked me into letting all the hurtful things out, talking about them, dealing with them for the first time. I feared what she would think of me once she had seen everything, and I was afraid to face the pain I knew was bound to surface. But Carla helped me realize that my family and life experiences have made me the individual I am, and that I have no reason to feel ashamed.

One night during my freshman year, I received a frantic call from home. The family was gathered at University Hospital in Newark. My oldest brother, Kenny, had been beaten in the head with some type of heavy blunt object—I heard it was a golf club—during a fight. He had lost a lot of blood, was unconscious, and would probably not survive. I rushed to his bedside and was devastated by what I saw. His bandaged head was hugely swollen, and his face was black and blue. He lay so still that he looked frozen. I couldn't stand seeing him that way and rushed out of the room. I had been angry at Kenny for years for drinking so much and causing such a disturbance at Moms's house. But he was my brother. I didn't want him to die.

I immediately began feeling guilty about being in college. None of my brothers or sisters had been given such an opportunity. What was so special about me? I might not have been able to prevent the fight that left my brother nearly dead, but if I had been working instead of going to college, I could at least have been helping Moms out with the bills. I was the one who had held our family together. My rep in the neighborhood had helped to protect them. When I left for college, I felt I had abandoned them. When I started college, Moms began collecting discarded aluminum cans off the sidewalks and streets during her four A.M. street-cleanings to sell to a company that made money by recycling. This just proved my point and made me feel worse. She sent me her small profits, which made me feel special and loved but also unworthy. With Kenny's injury, all those feelings of guilt and responsibility and worthlessness came rushing back.

The next morning, I went to see Carla.

"Listen, you can't feel like you're the reason this happened," she told me. "You had no control over this. You can't live your life forever trying to take care of your family and monitor your brothers and sisters."

She helped me plow through the pain to see that it was best for me to stay in college and complete my education.

Ultimately, Kenny recovered, though he was left paralyzed on his right side. He is confined to a wheelchair and lives in a home for the disabled. At first, it was difficult for me to visit him there, and I turned to Carla many more times. But the amazing thing is, Kenny seems to have found peace and purpose in his life, and we have developed the close bond I always wanted. He no longer drinks. He participates in the daily recreational activities at the center. And get this: he's even talking about going to college. He says watching me pursue my degrees inspired him.

Carla understood that the students in her program faced many distractions outside of school and needed more than just academic enrichment to survive the academic world. Whatever the need, she tried to meet it or find someone who could.

At the end of our freshman year, Carla refused to allow Rameck, George, or me to go back to our old neighborhoods for the summer. She didn't want us to return to the influences of old friends or the other dangers there. I had shown her a letter that one of the guys who had taken part in the armed robbery wrote me from jail. He accused me of ratting them out, and he threatened to "get" me. She arranged for us to live and work on campus during the summer.

When scholarship, loan, and grant money fell short for one of us, which seemed to be every semester, Carla scrambled to find other potential resources. When Rameck and I unexpectedly became the first students accepted into a new program that allowed us to enroll in the Robert Wood Johnson Medical School in Piscataway a year early, Carla stepped in to offer more emotional support to George, whom we had to leave behind.

Before Rameck and I left to begin medical school, the two of us and George visited Carla at her office to give her some pictures we had taken during our college graduation ceremony. She opened her purse and stuck the photos inside without paying much attention to where they landed. When she made it home, she took out her purse to look at the pictures again. She realized then that she had placed them inside the small burgundy leather Bible she carries with her. The pictures had landed on the Thirty-first Psalm, which ends this way:

*O love the Lord, all ye his saints: for the Lord preserveth*
*the faithful, and plentifully rewardeth the proud doer.*
*Be of good courage, and he shall strengthen your heart, all*
*ye that hope in the Lord.*

She took that as a sign. The good Lord would protect and keep us the rest of the way. Then, as my mother had done so many years earlier with the curly black braids she retrieved from the barber's floor after my first haircut, Carla placed the graduation photos back inside her Bible and closed it.

She has kept us in there ever since.

# 10

A DIFFERENT WORLD

*Rameck*

MY FRESHMAN YEAR at Seton Hall was like living in a foreign country where few people looked like me or spoke my
language. And the trouble started right away.

I had been on campus just half a semester when I invited
my stepbrother Michael to visit me. I called him my stepbrother, but he was really the son of my father's longtime girlfriend. Michael had dropped out of high school, and I hoped
that exposing him to college life would encourage him to
return. In elementary school he had been a smart kid who
made straight A's, wore glasses, and loved to read. The kids at
school, in his neighborhood, and even in his family had called
him a nerd and teased him mercilessly. I teased him, too. But
as we got older, I felt bad for him. I knew he was a good guy,
and I could see the teasing was really bothering him. His
grades fell. He began hanging out with troublemakers and

eventually just stopped going to school. He began working out in the gym and transformed his once-scrawny frame into muscles and mass. Before long, he was getting into trouble, too.

He accepted the invitation to visit me at Seton Hall, and he brought one of his cousins and another friend with him. They ran wild on campus all day. About one o'clock the next morning they were still at it, making too much noise in Bolden Hall, the freshman dormitory where I lived. I was afraid they would get us all into trouble, so I confronted Michael in the hall outside my room on the third floor. He accused me of making a big deal out of nothing. My temper blew, and we began arguing loudly, as though we were about to fight. A crowd of students gathered around us, ready to watch some kind of showdown. All of a sudden, I looked up and saw a bunch of white faces staring at us. I felt ashamed. We were a spectacle, confirming white folks' worst stereotypes.

Most of my encounters with white folks at that point in my life had been negative: white sales clerks following me through stores on shopping trips to the mall, white police officers stopping and harassing me on the streets of my neighborhood, white passengers holding on to their purses a bit tighter on the train when I passed them. To the average white stranger, I was an instant security threat, a thug, an object to be loathed or feared, not a human being with a heart and dreams and family and fears. I resented the stereotype.

But instead of calming myself down, I turned my anger on the crowd.

"Why don't y'all get away from here," I shouted. "We're

just having a little disagreement. This ain't nothing for y'all. We ain't no spectacle."

The crowd dispersed, all but two white guys, who continued to stare. One of them wore an arrogant smirk.

"Y'all didn't hear what I said," I yelled. "I said, 'Leave'!"

The one with the smirk stood his ground.

"Well, we live on this floor, too. We pay tuition, too, and we don't have to go anywhere."

My anger rose another notch.

"What did you say?" I asked, feigning disbelief, staring him dead in his eyes, trying to intimidate him to back down.

He repeated himself, full of that righteous, white-boy attitude.

Now my stepbrother and his boys were looking at me as if to say, "Man, this white boy is getting the best of you. What you gonna do?" If I did nothing, I'd look like a punk.

I walked over to him and stood chest to chest.

"Look, I'm counting to three. If you don't leave, you gonna wish you had."

The white boy chuckled a bit in my face, then turned to his partner.

"He's trying to threaten us. Humph, like I really care."

I couldn't believe this white boy was disrespecting me. Mind you, he was right. He had as much claim to the hallway space as I had, and I had no business ordering him to his room. But my mind was too filled with anger to accept a rational thought. All I saw was an arrogant white boy trying to put me in my place.

I slowly counted to three. The white boy didn't move.

With a strength that belied my small frame, I grabbed him simultaneously by his collar and his crotch, raised him over my head, and dropped him. He slammed to the floor, head first. His neck bent in an odd way, and his body fell limp.

Fear replaced my anger. For a few seconds, all I could hear was my heart thumping wildly. I thought I had paralyzed or killed the guy.

Suddenly, he moved.

I exhaled.

But with my stepbrother and his boys watching, I couldn't drop my tough-guy demeanor.

"Now, get up," I commanded.

The boy was silent. His friend helped him up, and he limped away.

I turned and walked past my stepbrother and his boys to my room. I fell on my bed. Sam was out that night, and George was across the hall in his suite. I lay in my room alone, thinking to myself over and over: Man, what have you done? What have you gotten yourself into now?

About four A.M., loud banging on the door of my suite broke my sleep.

"South Orange Police," a voice yelled from the other side.

They had come for me. I resigned myself to what was sure to happen next. The white boy would press charges against me. I would get kicked out of school. And for what? Because the white boy didn't leave when I told him to leave? I was wrong, and I knew it. I just hadn't been thinking about the consequences. On the streets where I grew up, you didn't worry about consequences. If someone disrespected you, you beat his ass. Period.

From the time I was a little boy, my mother had warned me never to come home crying because I was scared to fight back when someone picked on me.

"If you don't beat his ass, don't come home crying," she said. "If you do, I'm gonna beat your ass. Either way, you get an ass-whuppin'. So, who do you want it from?"

I opened the door to my suite and followed the officers to a small room downstairs. The dormitory director was there with the boy and his parents.

"Is this the guy?" the officer asked, pointing at me.

"Yes, that's him," the boy responded.

"Do you want to press charges?" the officer asked, seeming much too eager.

The boy didn't respond. His mother looked at me. I expected anger, but there was none.

"No, we don't want to press charges against him," she said softly. "That's okay."

I looked at her with eyes that asked: "You don't?" I figured that's what they had come to do. Maybe she knew I would get kicked out of school if she pressed charges, and she didn't want to ruin my life. I don't know. But now the officer was telling me I was free to go. I wanted to thank her, but I was too shocked to speak.

Her decision didn't end the matter, though. Because the incident had occurred on campus, I was summoned to appear before a board of university administrators who would decide my fate.

The next day, my two white suitemates approached me. Sam and I had been cordial to them, but we mostly kept our distance. They said they had heard what happened and wanted to know if there was anything they could do to help. One of them said his father was a lawyer and could represent me if I needed help. I thanked him for such a kind gesture, but I didn't really need an attorney.

On the day of the hearing, I walked into the room, and about a half dozen administrators, mostly white men, sat around a long wooden table. One of them, a priest with deep blue eyes and white hair, looked particularly sinister. The white boy was there with his foot in a cast. His foot had slammed to the ground with such force that a bone had snapped. I was sure the administrators, after taking one look at him, would kick me out of school no matter what I had to say.

They called me to testify. I explained what had happened and apologized to the guy I had hurt. I truly regretted what I had done. I presented supportive letters from one of my professors and Carla Dickson, who pleaded for mercy on my behalf. The administrators conferred with one another and announced their decision. They would give me another chance. They put me on probation for six months. If I got into any more trouble during that time, I would be expelled immediately.

Silently, I thanked God.

The mother's decision not to press charges against me had probably influenced the board. The compassion she displayed touches me still. It challenged the deep distrust I felt at the time toward white folks. How could I continue to feel that way when this mother, who had every right to be angry that I had hurt her son, chose compassion instead? And when the administrators, who would have been justified in kicking me out, chose mercy? And when my suitemates, whom I had avoided most of the time, offered their help? I was, like, "Wow, there are some really cool white people in the world."

I recognized that I needed to change. If I let my best friends down and blew this opportunity to get a college education, I could blame no one but myself. I prayed to God:

"Lord, I know I got to get my act together 'cause sooner or later you're gonna stop looking out for me."

I'm glad God is patient, because before the end of my freshman year, I wound up in trouble again.

Sam and I were in the room studying one day when some guys I knew stopped by for a visit. They were all dressed in Seton Hall sweatshirts and pants, and they bragged about how easy it was to steal them from the campus bookstore. I knew security in the store was lax, because earlier that year I had stolen a textbook I needed for class. I had run out of money, couldn't call home for help, and was feeling desperate. This time, greed was the motivation.

I walked alone to the bookstore in the basement of one of the lecture halls and went straight to the rack where the sweatshirts were hanging. The store was empty except for the sales clerk behind the counter. There were a bunch of empty hangers, and one large sweatshirt left. I scanned the store quickly with my eyes to make sure no one was watching me. Then I slipped the sweatshirt off the rack, stuck it under my shirt, and casually browsed around the store for several minutes. I thought about buying a pen or something cheap to lessen any possible suspicion, but I changed my mind at the last minute. As I passed the front counter on my way out, I felt the eyes of the sales clerk on me.

"Excuse me," he said in the most nasal, annoying tone. "What do you have under your shirt?"

"What are you talking about?" I responded, trying to sound offended.

"You have to come with me," he said.

I couldn't believe that this sales clerk, just another student, was challenging me. I took off running.

"Hey, come back here," I thought I heard him say.

I dashed up the basement steps and toward an open field. I was sure I had gotten away. But when I glanced behind me, I was shocked to see the clerk, a tall guy with long, lanky legs, following my trail. I pumped my legs harder, but I was quickly running out of breath. I made it to President's Hall, the administration building, pulled out the sweatshirt, and stashed it behind some bushes. At least if I got caught, I wouldn't have the stolen merchandise on me.

I took off running again toward Bolden Hall. I glanced back, and the clerk was still chasing me. After about ten minutes of running at full speed, I made it to my dorm. Another student was swiping his identification card to open the electronic doors. I rushed in behind him and ran down the hall to a friend's room. When she opened her door, I burst in and closed the door quickly behind me.

"What's wrong?" she asked, startled.

I said I'd tell her later and asked if I could just sit for a while.

I was too scared even to talk anymore. Sweat dripped from my face like rain. I sat at my friend's desk, closed my eyes, and cradled my head in my hands. My conscience whipped me. I was still on probation. If the sales clerk found me, I would be kicked out of Seton Hall for sure. I had gambled with my future for a lousy sweatshirt. How could I be so stupid? There would be no more chances. Sam and George would have to go on without me.

I kept waiting for the knock on the door. The clerk had chased me this far, I didn't think he would give up until he nabbed me. Surely someone had seen me slip into my friend's room.

Forty-five minutes passed. I sent my friend into the hall to see if anyone was searching for me. Several people told her that a guy from the bookstore had been walking up and down the halls asking residents if they had seen anyone who fit my description. But he was gone. The hall was quiet.

I needed some fresh air. I also still wanted that sweatshirt. Part of me felt—crazily—justified in trying to keep it since I had gone through such trouble to get it. I walked outside and headed back across the field to President's Hall. My stash was gone. The sales clerk must have found it and taken it back to the store.

As I walked back to my dorm, I got the feeling that I had just used my last chance. My mind quickly crowded with thoughts. I couldn't keep risking everything. College was different from anything I had ever known, but I could get so much out of it if I just tried. I was making good grades, which meant I was smart enough to be here. All I had to do was stay out of trouble. If I got kicked out of college, where would I go? Back to Ma's house? That would surely break her heart. And what would happen to Sam and George?

I thought about my old friends in Plainfield. Of the ten of us, only three had even graduated from high school. And I was the only one in college. The walk back to my dorm seemed to take forever. But I'm certain I grew up that day.

I finally realized that if I wanted to change my life, I had to act differently. I stopped stealing. I worked extra hours. One summer I even got a second job to help buy my books, school supplies, and personal items. Sam, George, and I borrowed from one another. And when that still wasn't enough, I just did without things I needed or wanted.

When I told Sam and George what had happened, we laughed it off. Sam never said, "I told you so," though he had chosen to stay in the room when I left for the bookstore. By watching him and George, I began to see that I didn't have to act so tough to be cool, and I tried harder to control my temper.

I can't say I was successful right away. I got into more fights, and I blew up more times than I would have liked. But with time and a conscious effort to think about the consequences before I responded, I slowly evolved into a different person.

I rarely took time to read anything other than books assigned for class. But at a book sale my freshman year, one provocative title caught my eye: *Countering the Conspiracy to Destroy Black Boys.*

I bought the book. When I read it, I saw myself for the first time.

I didn't realize then that the same book had inspired Carla, my college counselor. In it, Jawanza Kunjufu explains that many black boys turn to the streets to learn how to become men because they don't have fathers at home and no one steps in to fill the void. He discusses the importance of reaching black boys before they are hardened by the ways of the street and build a rap sheet the length of a football field.

I knew firsthand that he was right, and I immediately wanted to help.

All my life I had been taught that black folks have a responsibility to help one another out. I heard it when I followed my uncles to gatherings of the Nation of Islam. And Bill, the owner of the barbershop where I worked as a teenager, preached the same message.

Bill owned a small, three-chair shop that sat on Front Street, across from the Anchor Bar, the corner store, and Steve's Record Shop. He was in his forties when I worked for him, and he fit the mold of the stereotypical barber: opinionated and quick to dispense advice. He and the other barbers kept the place packed with men of all ages who seemed to enjoy sitting around debating the issues of the day as much as getting a haircut. The men engaged in typical barbershop banter about sports, women, and politics. But when the crowd left and Bill and I prepared the shop for closing, I'd sweep up puddles of hair while Bill sat in his chair and pitched questions my way: Why did I think people in the neighborhood were so poor? What could I do to help? What did I think about God? What did the schools teach me about George Washington? Did I know he owned slaves?

I was just thirteen, but Bill pushed me to question things and to think about issues I hadn't considered before. In high school I even envisioned myself as an activist. But I never saw the dichotomy of that side of myself and the other side that stayed in trouble and did harmful things to people. I didn't think I was a bad person, but I kept doing bad things.

When I read Kunjufu's book, I began to see myself more clearly, and I tried harder to change. I've always been a hyper, energetic person, so as soon as I read the book I immediately wanted to act. I came up with an idea to start a mentoring program for kids in poor neighborhoods. I went to Sam and George. The three of us started brainstorming. We could recruit other volunteers, identify schools in Newark, and become mentors to the students there. We could even sponsor bus trips to bring students to Seton Hall so they could see a college campus, perhaps for the first time.

We wanted to do for children what we knew would have helped us.

The three of us approached the Student Government Association, which ordains and finances official campus organizations. But the association was not eager to sanction a new group. The officers said we needed a faculty sponsor and a proposal before they could even consider our idea. They suggested we implement our program through an existing black organization.

Nothing motivates Sam, George, and me more than being told "No." We quickly found a sponsor, Professor Forrest Pritchett, an assistant professor in the African American Studies department. Then we sat down together and put our ideas into a proposal. But what would we call our organization?

In his book, Kunjufu discusses the principles of Kwanzaa. One of them seemed to fit: Ujima, which in Swahili means "collective work and responsibility." I suggested it to George and Sam. They loved it.

We went back to the SGA. This time the officers gave in, but they awarded us a measly $500. They said we had to raise whatever else we needed. I have to admit that we were pissed. We had grandiose ideas, and we thought that just maybe some folks on our campus didn't want a bunch of black kids from the inner city spending time at the university. That thought motivated us more. We set out to raise some money.

During another brainstorm, we came up with a fund-raising idea. We could throw a big party in the student union. We were an official campus organization, so we had access to the university's facilities free of charge. Since we always went to other nearby campuses to have fun because few parties at Seton Hall played black music, we figured we could charge the standard $5, advertise big, and draw students from the colleges and universities we frequented.

I don't remember who came up with the theme for the party, but it was perfect: Ujima Jam.

By then, George, Sam, and I were sophomores. We had never thrown a big party before, but we had been around enough to know that the d.j. was the key to success. We needed somebody who knew just what to play and when. One of us remembered that a friend of ours from high school was dating a popular d.j. around Newark. We called her, and she helped us book him at a discount rate.

Next, Sam, George, and I used the computer to make fliers. Each of us took a bunch and drove to different campuses within an hour's drive—Rutgers, Drew, Fairleigh Dickinson, and others—to spread the news. We walked around handing our fliers to other students and placing them on car windows. We distributed at least 1,000 fliers.

The problem with throwing a party like this, though, was that we had no idea until the night of the gig whether it would be a success. That night, the three of us got there early to meet the d.j. We had asked other volunteers to collect the money at the door because we had too many friends who we knew would try to get in free if they saw one of us standing there.

I watched the door all night, and within the first two hours, we had packed the house. After expenses, we cleared several hundred dollars. The party was such a success that we threw another one and sold soda and chips.

We chose two elementary schools in Newark. George, Sam, and I recruited a few other students and began visiting the schools at the end of the day at least once a week to tutor students and talk to them about college. But when we approached the principals about busing the kids to campus, we got a luke-warm response and ultimately got bogged down in discussions about liability.

We were just nineteen years old when we planned our

organization, so we naively thought that recruiting mentors and bringing kids to campus would be simple. We thought other students would be knocking on our doors to help and that public-school officials would bend over backward to provide kids with this opportunity. We learned real fast that we were wrong.

We continued to mentor at the schools we had chosen, but it seemed that one of the biggest components of our organization—bringing kids to campus—had failed. Somehow, though, a teacher from a school in Brooklyn heard about our organization and contacted us. She wanted to bring a group of students from her school to campus. We were eager to work with her.

The school itself bused the students to campus and provided chaperones. Ujima bought lunch for all of the students and gave them a tour of the campus, and a few volunteers spoke to them about college life.

Just seeing the excitement in the eyes of the kids as they explored the campus made me feel that I was doing something worthwhile.

I can't remember ever feeling more proud of myself.

Rameck on

# GIVING BACK

I discovered early in my childhood that you don't need money or status to enrich another person's life. Anybody with passion and purpose can do so.

Throughout my life, people have given generously of their time, skills, money, and more to help me succeed. They all had busy lives, and they didn't owe me a thing. Yet they gave. I've always believed in the old adage that says much is required of those to whom much is given. So I've always felt compelled to give back.

George, Sam, and I believe strongly that God protected us and lifted us up so that we could become examples to kids today—especially kids growing up in poor communities—of what is possible for them. That's why we started the mentoring program called Ujima in our freshman year of college, and, more recently, the Three Doctors Foundation.

The ways to give are as boundless as your creativity. Maybe you're a nurturer and can mentor a younger or less-experienced colleague on the job. Maybe you're good with children and can spend a few extra hours a week reading or tutoring kids at your local elementary school. Or maybe you have the cash to send a kid in your neighborhood to summer camp or to buy groceries for a poor family during the holidays.

Giving is like playing a position on a football team. Everybody can't be the quarterback. You may be better at linebacker, wide receiver, or water boy. The important thing is that you find your position, whatever it is, and play hard.

As a teenager, I lacked the one person in my life who could have made a difference earlier—a male mentor, a respectable father figure who would have been willing to spend time with me consistently, giving me advice and sharing fun things to keep me away from the bad influences in my neighborhood. I believe that most boys, regardless of who they are or where they live, long for that kind of relationship with a father, a big brother, or even a stranger who steps in to fill the void. And that desire for male guidance stays with us from childhood, when our lives are taking shape, to adulthood, when we are making crucial decisions about careers, life, and family.

George always says that people should give even if they are selfish because there are selfish reasons to give. Your gift might touch the life of a kid who otherwise might end up breaking into your house, jacking your car, or selling drugs to your child. Or your gift might help to raise the brain surgeon who someday saves your life. I'm not trying to scare anyone, but the point is that there is no excuse not to give, even if your reason is a selfish one. But there is another selfish reason to give: when you give to someone else, I've found, surprisingly, that you often receive as well.

In college, I discovered that when I went to elementary schools to tutor kids, I received as much as or more than the children did. We live in an age of excess, in which a person's value is attached to how much money he makes, what kind of car she drives, how many things have been acquired. But no monetary value can be placed on the feeling that comes when you know you've made a difference in another person's life. And all of us could use a boost in self-esteem—especially teenage boys, who can often be too macho to admit that they need a good pat on the back.

And don't forget—when you touch another person's life, the gift keeps on multiplying. Consider George's third-grade teacher. She couldn't have known then that by making a difference in George's life, she someday would also make a difference in Sam's and mine.

# 11

## RAP

### *George*

RAP MUSIC DEFINED our generation the way the Motown sound had defined our parents' era.

We pumped up our music to get in the mood for studying and when we wanted to celebrate. We partied to rap music. We chilled to it. And in our freshman year, Rameck and I stumbled into the creative side of it.

It started with a video-game competition. After class, Rameck and I often teamed up against two guys from Boston to play video games, mostly Sega Genesis basketball. One day, we turned on some music and started rapping back and forth, the two of us against the two of them. We'd alternately make up rhymes on the spot that chopped up the other players or their hometown. It was all in fun to determine who could come up with the cleverest lyrics.

Later on, Rameck and I challenged each other.

"Man, I'm better than you," one of us would brag.

And the contest began. Sometimes, we just rapped back and forth to each other in the room before going out to a party on a Thursday or Friday night. We even recorded a rap video once when a video company called Fun Flicks came to Seton Hall as part of a campus fun day. The company set up a booth with the latest high-tech equipment and offered students a chance to make a music video for free. We could choose from a list of songs and lip-synch to a recording while the cameraman added a creative backdrop, like stars. It was video karaoke. There were a few popular rap songs on the list, so Rameck and I got together with about five other friends and made several flicks.

One of the guys with us that day was a seasoned rapper known around campus as P.S. One night, Rameck and I were talking when one of us suggested that we try to hook up with P.S. to form a rap group. We approached him about it, and I was surprised that he agreed right away, because his skills were so far superior to ours. At first, we considered asking P.S. to write our lines, but we quickly realized that just wouldn't work. To feel what we were saying, each of us had to write our own lines. I became pretty good at coming up with metaphors, and Rameck developed great producer instincts. He was the one who pulled our individual pieces together into one good rap. We began by rapping over other groups' beats, then Rameck started creating beats for us using a friend's sampler. Sampling was a popular technique in which musicians lifted a particular sound, say a horn solo or drum beat, from a recorded song and pieced it with other samples or original beats to create background music.

We chose the name A.R.T., Another Rough Tribe, for our group in the tradition of the colorful rappers whose sole purpose was to have fun stringing words together, showcasing their talents, and bragging about their exploits, particularly with women. We were big fans of rap pioneers like KRS-One and Rakim, and others, like A Tribe Called Quest and Leaders of the New School, whose star, Busta Rhymes, broke away and became a popular solo rapper, sporting flashy, almost clownish costumes. We enjoyed listening to all kinds of rap, especially socially conscious rap and even gangsta rap, which ignited major controversy with its violent images and themes.

We were just having fun in our spare time, unsure of how far we wanted to go with the group. But gradually, we got more serious. We asked Sam to be our manager. He's always been more interested in working behind the scenes in rap and envisioned himself more as a business mogul, like Russell Simmons, or a producer, like Sean "Puffy" Combs.

The more we practiced, the better we got. We wanted to go into the studio to put together some original beats and record some songs, but we had no money. That's when a friend gave one of our tapes to her boyfriend, a Seton Hall basketball star who was being recruited to play in the NBA. An agent he knew owned a big studio in Newark, so he arranged for us to get some free studio time. We went to the studio at least once a week, sometimes more often, depending on our class schedules, and recorded a couple of raps. But after a while, the studio wanted to start charging us, so we had to come up with another plan.

Sam came to our rescue. Always a penny-pincher, Sam had some extra money from his savings over the years and decided to front us $500. Since all three of us were struggling financially, we recognized the huge sacrifice he was making. There was no guarantee that he would get his money back, and, unlike me, he couldn't call home for help with his tuition when his money ran short. When I made it to college, my mother took on part-time jobs, in addition to her full-time job at the insurance company, and sent every dime of the extra money to me to help with tuition and books. She would have killed me if I had used even a penny of it to pursue a career as a rapper. But Sam understood our passion, believed in our talents, and decided to gamble.

We found another studio owned by Kool and the Gang, a funk band popular in the 1970s, went in, and recorded a couple more songs. We also heard that the Fugees, popular at the time with lead vocalist Lauryn Hill, had a studio in East Orange called the Booga Basement. When we stopped by, we hit it off with the cousin of Wyclef Jean, one of the group's founders. Wyclef's cousin ran the studio and told us he would put together some beats for us. We only had to pay for studio time. We used the Booga Basement to cut three more songs, which were even better than our first ones.

Now we were ready to copyright our material, but we mistakenly thought we would have to hire a lawyer. Rameck came up with an alternative, the so-called poor man's copyright: we typed the lyrics of our songs, and he sent a copy of them via certified mail to himself. When we had four or five songs on a demo tape, we decided to put together a package to send to record companies. We didn't have enough money for professional photos, so Rameck asked a guy who took pictures for the student newspaper to take a promotional photo of us.

To look like real rappers, we had to appear tough, not like the college boys we had become. We scouted the campus for the perfect photo background. The green grass and stately trees surrounding Seton Hall just wouldn't do. Finally, we found the perfect spot: the upper deck of the student parking lot. The bare look of the concrete at night and the three of us in our baggy jeans, bad-boy expressions, and hats flipped backward looked just about right.

By now, we were in our junior year of college. We assembled thirty packets, each containing a copy of the demo, a promotional photo, and a short bio crafted by our wordsmith, P.S. Then, we used the telephone book and directory assistance to track down the addresses and telephone numbers of about twenty record companies. We were ready for New York. Rameck, P.S., and I skipped our classes and spent a day there, distributing our material. Rameck drove his white Volkswagen Golf, and each of us chipped in for gas and parking. We went from one record company to the next and handed our packet to the highest-ranking person available. A few times we were asked to drop our tape in a box with hundreds of others.

One of the record companies on our list was Puffy's Bad Boy Records. Puffy had just started the label with a guy named Harve Pierre. Directory assistance had given us a Harlem

address. But when we drove up, we didn't see any office buildings. The address was an apartment complex in the middle of
the 'hood. For a moment, we sat, perplexed, in the car. What
should we do? You don't just go walking up to some apartment in the 'hood without knowing where you're going. Anything could happen. But we had come this far. We weren't
turning around.

We found a telephone and called the number on our list.
Sure enough, it was Bad Boy Records. We asked the person
answering the telephone to confirm the address. He gave us
an apartment number. We walked up to the door and rang the
buzzer. A voice answered.

"Is this Bad Boy Records?" one of us asked.

"Yeah, come on up."

We felt a bit awkward when we first walked into the apartment because a bunch of guys were just sitting around. We
looked around the room. No Puffy.

"What do you need?" one of the guys asked.

We explained that we were rappers and wanted Puffy to
listen to our tape. We figured we had a better chance of getting called back if we could get Puffy to listen to it on the
spot. Puffy wasn't there, but we were directed to a bedroom,
where Harve Pierre, Puffy's vice president, sat on a king-sized
bed surrounded by at least 300 tapes. Three different phones
sat on the bed next to him, and he had one at each ear. He
looked up and saw us.

"Can I help y'all? What do you need?"

With each of us speaking at different times, we told him

we were rappers, that we were in college at Seton Hall, and we really wanted him to listen to our tape.

"That's cool, man. That's dope," he responded with a friendliness that immediately put us at ease. He chatted with us for about five minutes, but he said he was too busy to listen to the tape right then. He asked us to put it in his pile, and he promised to call us back.

We left, feeling super-hyped. We were sure we would hear from Bad Boy Records. Puffy was just getting started and surely must have been looking for new artists like us. But the telephone call from Bad Boy Records never came. We didn't get even one response from the twenty packets we distributed. We kept trying. We started getting weekend gigs.

Our first big performance was at a nightclub about fifteen minutes from Seton Hall. It was a hip-hop club that drew a young adult crowd, mostly college students of all races, who came to dance and watch live performances. When we made it to the club the night of our gig, customers were lined up outside the door to get in. As V.I.P.s, we bypassed the crowd. That made us feel important. We did a sound check, gave the disc jockey our instrumental tape, and chilled in the back of the club, near the bar, until it was time to go on stage. We were the opening act.

"What's up, y'all? How y'all doing out there?" Rameck yelled into the microphone as the crowd gathered around the makeshift stage. He introduced himself, then me, then P.S. by our stage names.

"I'm the Old Veteran. This is Sound Seeker, and this is

O.Z., the Wizard. And we're Another Rough Tribe. . . .
Alright, d.j., drop that beat!"

The bass began pounding, and we were into our first song,
getting the crowd hyped and dancing to our beat.

*"Yo, check it out, check it out, check it out!"*

Bodies bounced in rhythm, and dozens of white, yellow,
brown, and black hands pumped in the air. They loved us.

"Aw, man, y'all are dope. When's your CD coming out?"
one person after another asked afterward.

For the moment, we were hot and loving it.

I gave one of our packets to Faith Evans, my friend from
elementary school. Through her, Rameck, Sam, and I met
some of the guys who would become rap megastars. One of
them was Biggie Smalls, also known as The Notorious B.I.G.,
whom Faith had married in 1994, just days after they'd met at
a photo shoot for Bad Boy Records. For a while she lived in
East Orange and sometimes invited me to her house with
them for Sunday dinner. Biggie was a huge dude who must
have weighed more than 300 pounds. I'll never forget the
image of him seated at the kitchen table with a mound of
chicken bones piled high on his plate. He had devoured the
fried chicken at record speed.

Faith was the first female artist signed by Bad Boy Records
in 1994, and I went to the recording studio with her every
chance I got while she was working on her first album. I'd sit
on the floor while Faith recorded in the booth. Puffy, Biggie,
and other stars would be in and out all the time. Everybody
was down-to-earth, just regular people back then.

Once, Faith invited Sam, Rameck, and me to a photo shoot

at Bad Boy Records. The three of us were rolling dice in a small bathroom when Biggie walked in and put up $100. He lost it to Sam in a game called Celo. Biggie put up another $100 and lost that, too. He kept betting until he owed Sam more than $3,000. Few guys could roll better than Sam. They kept playing until he won all but $400 of it back. But $400 was a big deal to a broke college student.

Biggie and Puffy raised the profile of rap on the East Coast, especially in New York City. Biggie had been a crack dealer in Brooklyn, and he crafted complex rhymes with lurid lyrics that painted vivid images of the realities of inner-city life—the harshness of it, but also the glitzy style that came to be known as ghetto-fabulous. Some of his lyrics were disrespectful to women, but mostly Biggie just wanted to make you feel good and tell you how he was loving life. When you listened to him, you were living the glamorous life through him.

At the same time, Biggie's West Coast rival, Tupac Shakur, was also selling millions of records with more introspective and poetic lyrics that delved into the life and soul of the gangsta. Even if you weren't from the inner city, if you listened to Tupac, you got the feeling that the thugs have more heart than you thought. He reached into himself and tried to interpret where a lot of the negative behavior came from, and he crafted his lyrics in a way that you could really understand.

I knew the world they rapped about, and I was a fan of both rappers. But their rivalry ultimately escalated into an East Coast–West Coast feud that, some say, took the lives of rap's top two stars. Tupac was shot to death on September 7, 1996, in a drive-by shooting in Las Vegas. Six months later, Biggie was gunned down as he left an after-party for the Soul Train Music Awards. The attackers were never identified in either shooting.

I was hoping tensions would cool after Tupac's death, so when Biggie died less than a year later in almost the same way, I was shocked. My phone rang off the hook with friends calling to mourn, as if a blood brother had just been murdered. Big, tough dudes in my old neighborhood were walking around dazed. I was sure the anti-rap forces would find a way to put more pressure on the rap industry and just shut it down. Critics were already blaming rap for glorifying and perpetuating the violence in communities like the ones where Sam, Rameck, and I grew up.

By the time Biggie was killed, Rameck and I had already made a major decision about our career as rappers.

When we gave the tape to Faith in 1994, our junior year in college, she passed it on to her lawyer, who sent it to Dennis Scott, an NBA player who was with the Orlando Magic. He owned a company called 3D Entertainment, which managed a couple of rap groups. Apparently he liked one of our songs, and he sent us a letter saying he wanted to hear more. The problem was, we were flat broke. We didn't have the resources to go back into the studio and record.

Rameck was so excited about our chances of succeeding as rappers that he wanted to put everything into making this dream happen. He was even willing to skip medical school. He figured the three of us would still be together, just pursuing a different dream. But the life of a rapper was *his* dream, not ours. He loved the stage, the spotlight, and the cheers from the crowd. It was part of his fantasy of becoming an actor. To him, being a rapper was the next-best thing. We had good connections, and he figured we could count on them for help, and if things didn't work out, we could always return to school.

I wasn't feeling the same way. Graduation from college was less than a year away, and we had to start applying to dental and medical schools. We had to make a crucial decision. One night, the subject came up during conversation.

"Yo, man, we can really do this," Rameck began. "Let's just do it. Let's go and be rappers."

It was time for me to be honest. My enthusiasm was waning. I knew that if I gave my books enough time, I was guaranteed to become a dentist. But I could go into the studio a million times, and no matter how good the songs were, I wasn't guaranteed to sell those records. With rap, it really came down to luck. Maybe we would be some of the lucky ones. But I wasn't willing to take that risk.

"Look, how many broke rappers are out there, man?" I said to Rameck. "One day they're big and hot with the biggest studio, and the next day, they're not. Man, you're on your way to medical school. You want to drop medical school for this? I'm on my way to dental school. I'm not dropping dental school for this. You're crazy."

"Come on, man. You're stupid, man. Let's just try. Let's just see what happens," Rameck shot back.

I didn't budge.

"Naw, man, I'm not even gonna see," I said. "At some point, we'd still have to make a decision, and I've already made mine."

Rameck got quiet. I had just spewed acid on his fantasy, and it was shriveling up before his eyes. He didn't want to try it alone, and P.S., our other partner, had already drifted away. P.S. was a brilliant student, as talented in math as he was in rap, but he didn't try hard at either one and ended up dropping out of Seton Hall.

After a few minutes of silence, Rameck looked at me. I wasn't sure what he would say.

"*You know what, man?*" he said softly. "*You're right.*"

That was it. Our career as rappers came to an abrupt halt. Our pact was still solid. Once again, we were on our way to becoming doctors.

# 12

## LOVESICK

### *Rameck*

I ALWAYS THOUGHT I was too cool to let a girl break my heart.

Then I met the woman I'll call Kay. She was standing next to a friend of mine from high school after a party at Rutgers University in New Brunswick when I spotted her. She was so fine—on the tall side, with golden-brown skin, shoulder-length dark brown hair, innocent eyes, and a tempting smile.

"Who's your friend?" I asked my high-school friend.

She introduced me to Kay and told her flattering things about me. Kay was a freshman at Rutgers and was two years younger, but the chemistry between us was instant and powerful. She gave me her telephone number. When I called her the next day, we talked for nearly five hours straight.

From South Orange to New Brunswick was a long-distance call, so I rang up a huge telephone bill those first few weeks as Kay and I got to know each other. She and I started hanging out together regularly. Sometimes, we double-dated or triple-dated with Sam, George, and their dates. All of us would go out to dinner, to a party, or bowling. Once, the six of us even went ice skating in New York City's Rockefeller Center.

When Sam, George, or I had a girlfriend, she automatically became part of our group, like a little sister to the other two of us, and she was off-limits as a potential date. That's why we never had a conflict over a girl.

In the first few years of college, Sam and I played the field more than George, who more often than not had a steady girl-friend. Even though I played around, I always knew I wanted to get married and have children after college. I wanted to have the perfect family I had always hoped for as a kid. I didn't ever want to inflict the insecurity of a broken home—like the childhood I'd had—on a child. I tried to be careful. I couldn't have any baby-mama drama disrupting my dreams.

Things got serious pretty quickly between Kay and me, and we often talked about getting married and having kids together someday. I thought she was the one. But one night while I was visiting her in her dorm room at Rutgers, her tele-phone kept ringing. She seemed uneasy when she answered it, and she gave one-word answers, "Yes," or "No," and then "I'll have to talk to you later."

"Who was that?" I asked.

She wasn't in the mood for my questions. We argued about it, and I left. Later that night over the telephone, she told me the truth: she had another boyfriend. He was a football jock who attended college in Boston. He had been her high-school sweetheart, and though she didn't want to be with him anymore, she hadn't quite broken things off.

I was crushed. How could I ever trust her? How could she do this to me? How could she do this to us? I broke up with her.

I was miserable for a few weeks until we got back together. She promised me the guy was out of her life for good, but the trust issue kept coming up. If she wasn't in her room when I called, I questioned her extensively. If she ignored her telephone while I was there, I got suspicious. And I felt justified.

She knew she had to earn my trust again, and for a while she did all she could. She'd stay in her room all day instead of hanging out with her friends, just to prove to me that there was no other man in her life. She wanted me to trust her. But the questions and suspicions lingered.

We broke up and got back together a million times. When we split just before my senior year, it seemed like all the other times. I figured we would take some time to cool off and then in a week or two we would be a couple again. But I didn't realize that she had taken all she would take of my lack of trust. We were done, she kept telling me. At first, I didn't believe her. Then, I started hearing rumors that she was dating someone else. I confronted her. It was true.

My girl had moved on without me.

The guy she was dating was a legendary player. Everybody knew it. He had dated practically all of the pretty girls on Rutgers's campus, and all the others wanted him. Maybe it gave

Kay's ego a boost to be with him. But that's when it hit me that I could lose her for good.

I had heard the term "lovesick," and I figured it was something that happened to girls, certainly not to a tough guy like me. But all of a sudden, I couldn't sleep. I couldn't eat. I lost weight. I started calling Kay a dozen times a day trying to change her mind. I knew her new boyfriend didn't care for her the way I did.

I loved this girl. I wanted to marry her. I wanted to have kids with her. I had to get her back.

During one of those sleepless nights, a plan crystallized in my mind. Kay was the kind of woman who needed to be with her man all the time. I knew that once I began medical school, the workload would be so demanding that I wouldn't have time for her. Then, after medical school, I'd have to do a residency, which would keep me even busier. I would be nearly thirty years old before I had time for a wife and kids. At twenty-one, that seemed ancient. I decided I would just forget about medical school, marry Kay, and start our perfect family.

I knew I could get a job teaching.

Sam and I had arranged our schedules that semester to have a day off, on which we'd work as substitute teachers. I worked at a high school and elementary school in a community called Hillside. The principal of the elementary school had approached me one day and asked me my major.

"Biology," I told him.

"We need teachers," he said. "You're a young black man about to get a degree in biology. I have a job waiting for you when you finish."

I wondered how I would tell Sam and George that I was about to break the pact. We had promised to stick together to the end, but I figured they would be all right without me. I figured they would understand.

I had to live my own life.

I called Kay and asked to see her. She refused. I told her I loved her and needed her in my life. Then she told me what I had been dreading to hear: she was falling for the other guy, she wanted to try to make it work with him, and nothing I said could change her mind.

I never even got to tell her about my plan.

I was lovesick for months. I'm sure Sam and George noticed. But guys are proud. We don't even let our closest boys know if our heart is hurting.

"Naw, dog, I'm straight," I said when they asked about the weight loss.

I never told Sam or George about my plan, either. With my heart in pieces, I began preparing again for medical school.

# 13

# ACCESS MED

*Sam*

THE SUMMER BEFORE our senior year, Rameck and I got great news: we were the first Seton Hall students accepted into a new program designed to help minority students do better in medical school.

The program, Access Med, had begun a year earlier as a joint venture between the Robert Wood Johnson Medical School and Rutgers University. It was expanding to Seton Hall as we finished our junior year. As new participants, Rameck and I would be allowed to take half of our first-year medical-school courses while finishing our last year of college. That would leave us with a much lighter load, just half of the required courses, when we entered our first official year of medical school.

The first year is so daunting that large percentages of students drop out. Access Med was designed to make it easier for minority students, who are grossly underrepresented in medical schools, to survive that first year.

Rameck and I transferred to Rutgers for our senior year to be closer to the medical school. We spent the mornings at Robert Wood Johnson and the afternoons at Rutgers, taking the courses we needed to finish our senior year. The best part of taking the medical-school courses early was that if we passed, we would be accepted into Robert Wood Johnson without having to take the MCAT, the standardized test that medical schools use to decide who gets in. I was not looking forward to the MCAT. I didn't like the idea that my future could rest on a standardized test that I didn't believe could adequately gauge my intelligence or ability.

To qualify for Access Med, you had to have a minimum composite grade-point average of 3.2 on a 4.0 system over three years. I had a 3.6, and I would graduate from Seton Hall cum laude. I had received an A+ in organic chemistry, the make-or-break-you course in our field. That was practically unheard of for most of our students.

Rameck had a 3.4. Access Med participants also had to have completed all of the core courses in their majors by their senior year. The two of us needed only twelve hours, all electives, to graduate.

Dr. Linda Hsu, who had taught us biology, became our administrative link to Seton Hall, Rutgers, and Robert Wood Johnson. We had barely known her before then. But like Carla Dickson, she would adopt us and go far beyond her official duties to make sure we had everything we needed to succeed.

The only drawback of participating in Access Med was

that we had to leave George behind. With a grade-point average of 3.0, George had signed a letter of intent to enter dental school at the University of Medicine and Dentistry in Newark after graduation. I realized that Access Med was a great opportunity for Rameck and me, but I couldn't help feeling that we were abandoning George. So much of our success had been tied to our being together and supporting one another. But for the next few years, George would be on his own. And for the first time since the seventh grade, he and I would be separated for school.

Carla Dickson assured us that he would be fine.

"You've got to trust me," she said. "I've got George."

She began to call him every day.

Rameck and I packed up and headed to Rutgers in the fall of 1994. After moving several times, we landed in a small room on the second floor of a high-rise dormitory called the South Towers on the Livingston campus. The medical school operated on a different schedule, often remaining open when Rutgers was closed for long breaks. Each time Rutgers closed, we had to pack all of our belongings and move to another dorm.

Rameck and I were surprised to discover that Rutgers's Livingston campus—one of five campuses operated by the university—is predominantly black. When the two of us walked onto the yard for the first time, students were chilling in the lobby, listening to rap music, and playing cards. The scene felt instantly familiar and put us at ease. Rameck and I were always together, and when we went to the dining hall to eat, we could feel eyes on us. Other students were trying to figure us out. A guy everybody knew as Bam was one of the first students to approach us. We were headed down the steps of the dining hall one Friday night when he stopped us.

"What's up? Where y'all from?" he asked.

"Newark."

"Word? I'm from Irvington."

Irvington is on the border of Newark, so we instantly connected. Bam told us about a party that night, and the three of us hooked up and went together. Rutgers was a big party school, much larger and looser than Seton Hall. It reminded Rameck and me of New York, a stew of all kinds of people. The two of us and the guys who started hanging with us became one of the most popular cliques at school. Because we partied so much and were down-to-earth, other students couldn't believe it when we told them we were in medical school. I guess we didn't fit the traditional image of the medical student.

We established some lasting friendships on the Livingston campus. One day, Rameck and I were preparing to drive to Philadelphia for the "Greek," an annual weekend gathering of college students, most of them members of black fraternities and sororities. We stopped at a store and ran into another of the popular cliques, known for throwing some of the hottest parties at Rutgers. One of the cats walked up to me and introduced himself.

"Ain't you Sam?" he asked, then waited for my response. "My name is Sabu."

I was shocked because there was always underlying tension between the cliques on campus, but these brothers—

Sabu, Al-tareek, Rabu, Rad, Felix, Serron, J.P., and New—seemed different, really down-to-earth. I shot back the same vibe to him and told him how the ladies were always "biggin' them up." We bonded right then, went to the Greek together, and are cool to this day. Some of those guys are married and have children now, or are expecting them. Others never got married. When George, Rameck, and I started the Three Doctors Foundation, Sabu, Al-tareek, Al-tareek's brother, Dan, and Rabu donated $1,000, no questions asked.

I also fell in love on the Livingston campus. She walked into the dining hall one day and, wow, there was something about her that grabbed me right away. She was attractive, petite with a pecan-tan, earth-tone complexion, and had pretty, narrow brown eyes. I could tell by the way she walked that she was feisty. This might sound crazy, but I believed I saw a glow of light around her. Maybe it was that blue dress she was wearing, but I had to know who she was.

We quickly became a couple. It was so easy to vibe with her. She was one of the few people who really knew how to make me relax. Once, for my twenty-second birthday, she helped Rameck and George plan a surprise party for me at a club called Gregory's. It was my first birthday party since the kiddie parties my mom used to throw in the backyard.

During my second year of medical school, we broke up. Medical school was causing me such stress that even my relationship with her seemed to pull on me, and I broke away. She heard rumors that I was dating someone else, maybe because I happened to be with another girl when I ran into some of her relatives at Great Adventure theme park.

Months later, I realized how much I missed her and needed her in my life, and I stopped by the Livingston campus to look for her. But when I dropped by a friend's room first to get a haircut, he hit me with some shocking news.

"Hey, man, you heard about your girl?" he asked, referring to my former girlfriend. "She's four months pregnant!"

The news socked me in my gut. She and I hadn't been together during that time, so I knew the baby couldn't be mine. Even though I had broken up with her and knew I had hurt her, I felt betrayed for a long time. I clung to my friends.

Rameck and I often went to shoot hoops in the Livingston gym. One day, this cat from D.C. walked up to us and introduced himself. We knew he was from D.C. before he even said anything because the cats from D.C. always wore their socks pulled up to their knees, and with their shorts hanging down to their knees, all you could see was their kneecaps.

"Y'all got next?" he asked. "I'll run with y'all."

His name was Dax, and he would become our roommate the next year when he, Rameck, and I moved into a fabulous condominium complex called the Hampton Club. The place had two bedrooms, a loft, and a huge living room with cathedral ceilings and a spiral staircase. The complex was just five minutes from College Avenue and hadn't done as well commercially as expected, so the rent was cheap when split three ways. Dax volunteered to take the loft, and Rameck and I, as always, flipped a coin to determine who got the bigger room. We threw countless parties there, and George didn't miss a one. He usually spent the night. When he walked into our place, he knew he was home. He would kick off his shoes, go dig in the refrigerator, and then put his feet up like he lived there. We did the same when we went to his place. That's just how we were with one another.

George wasn't with us one time, though, when Rameck and I went to a club and ended up getting into a brawl together. I started dancing with a girl, not realizing she was already dancing with another guy.

"Yo, I'm dancing with her," he said, offended.

I ignored him. She started giving me more flavor than she gave him, and he walked away, looking defeated. One of my friends came up to me later and warned me that the guy had threatened to get me back for disrespecting him. I didn't think much about it, but when I got outside the club, about eight guys rushed me. I was in the middle of them throwing punches. All of a sudden I saw Rameck run into the circle and start throwing punches with me. He had my back.

Neither of us was seriously hurt, but Rameck got hit in the face and complained for days later that his jaw hurt. Years later when he got a dental X-ray, he learned that his jaw had been broken. I realized afterward that both of us could have gotten killed, and we tried to avoid such situations. But I always appreciated Rameck's loyalty.

Robert Wood Johnson was just a five-minute bus ride away. We took a class in biochemistry the first semester and classes in cell biology and histology the next. We rode the bus back to Rutgers in the afternoons for our electives. Traveling back and forth between the two schools wasn't so bad, once we caught the rhythm.

But medical school became a struggle for me right away.

I still liked to party too much and hadn't matured enough to realize that I couldn't hang out the same way anymore. Also, I still wasn't even sure I wanted to be a doctor. Those doubts had intensified in my sophomore year at Seton Hall when I witnessed a surgery for the first time.

Dr. Nathan Doctry, an African-American doctor and volunteer mentor for the Pre-Medical/Pre-Dental Plus Program, had invited me to accompany him during a knee surgery he was performing at East Orange Hospital. On the day of the surgery, I scrubbed up, followed him into the operating room, and watched as the anesthesiologist put the patient to sleep. Dr. Doctry then spliced holes in the patient's knee, inserted a scope, and began probing to find the problem.

"My goodness, that has got to hurt," I thought to myself.

Suddenly, I felt queasy, warm, and weak in the knees. I dashed over to the scrub sink. One of the nurses saw what was happening and yelled through the paper mask covering her mouth, "You can't do that there!"

It was too late. I hovered over the sink several minutes as my insides heaved involuntarily. Then I hung my head and slipped out of the operating room. I quickly composed myself and returned, but I wondered: How could I become a doctor if I couldn't even stand the sight of blood?

I just kept hoping my doubts would disappear once I entered medical school full-time. But at Robert Wood Johnson, I felt out of place. At first, I clung to Rameck and another Access Med student named Camille, who had also been an undergraduate at Rutgers. A math and science whiz-kid, Camille had skipped a couple of grades and entered college and medical school two years early. She and Rameck became friends first because, like him, she had grown up in Plainfield.

It seemed there was no one else on the medical-school campus I could identify with. When my colleagues talked about lifelong dreams of becoming a doctor, I felt guilty. I was in medical school, and though I knew I wanted to help people someday, I still wasn't sure I wanted to be a doctor.

Many of my colleagues had parents or other relatives who were doctors. In class, they were the ones who already knew how to use the medical instruments before our professors introduced them. They were the ones who nodded in agreement and raised their hands first during class lectures. And they were the ones who always knew the perfect companion books to buy or source to call for help when studying for a test. For me, everything was new, unfamiliar, and intimidating. Without the different summer programs I attended before our freshman and senior years of college, I would have been completely lost. I took notes furiously in class and occasionally scanned the room in a futile search for another face that showed even a hint of confusion, frustration, or fear. I'd never felt so alone.

A simple encounter during my third year of medical school pointed out clearly to me why more black children don't choose medicine as a career. They're just not exposed to it in an intimate way. You can't aim for what you can't see.

During a clinical rotation at the hospital where I worked, I stepped onto an elevator with a schoolmate who began talking about his weekend visit with a six-year-old niece. He said he had spent some time teaching her how to listen to the heart through a stethoscope and how to test the reflexes in the knees and arms with a reflex hammer. Can you imagine how comfortable she's going to feel with those same instruments if she ever decides to become a doctor? I was a twenty-three-year-old medical-school student the first time I held a stethoscope or even saw a reflex hammer. My only exposure to medicine as a child had been an occasional visit to a doctor's office or an emergency trip to the hospital.

Rameck didn't seem to struggle as much as I did. He loved science and math and seemed at peace with his decision. He, Camille, and I initially spent countless hours studying together. But Rameck and I studied differently. I was meticulous about going over facts and formulas over and over again until I was sure I understood every detail. That often slowed me down, but it didn't matter if I had to stay up practically all night to study for a big test. Rameck focused on understanding a concept, not the details, and usually was ready to move on to the next subject before I was. When he got tired, he was ready to call it quits. That would cause some tension between us later in medical school, and I would decide at times to study on my own.

We tried to balance the all-night study sessions in the library and dorm with some fun, though. This was, after all, our senior year of college, and the senior year is supposed to be fun. Between study sessions, Rameck and I played basketball in the recreation center, picked up George on the weekends, and went to parties. We often had to leave parties early when we had to study for a big test, but it seemed to relieve our frustration and stress if we partied for a few hours and left at a pre-set time. It was easier to walk away from the fun when I looked to my right and there was George, and I looked to my left and there was Rameck.

Because our medical-school classes required so much work, we were unable to hold part-time jobs, which meant we had no extra money coming in for books, food, and other necessities. Our student grants and loans only went so far. Most of that money paid for our tuition and our room and board.

One summer, Rameck worked two jobs. We were both hired as counselors for a high-school science program based at United Hospital in Newark, but Rameck also worked full-time at the Plainfield post office. He would work from eight A.M. to four P.M. at the hospital, return to our room at Seton Hall (where we stayed during the summer), sleep for a few hours, then go to work at the post office from eleven P.M. to seven A.M. He drove for forty-five minutes, straight from the post office to the hospital, and started it all again every day.

Our most fun job was as toll collectors on the New Jersey Turnpike during weekends, summers, and other long breaks from school. Sometimes, during our junior year, Rameck and I stayed out all night partying, then went home and put on our uniforms—navy-blue pants, gray shirts, and a matching navy-blue jacket in the winter—and made it to work for our six-thirty A.M. to two-thirty P.M. shift.

We initially worked different exits, but George transferred to the Jersey City exit, 15E, where Rameck worked. I worked at 16W, the exit to Giants Stadium. Rameck and George requested booths next to each other and talked across lanes the entire shift. They brought portable radios and CD players to work and swapped discs back and forth. All three of us brought our books and studied during down time. The two of them rode to work together and stopped every morning at the Dunkin Donuts for a box of Munchkins and coffee. George, who hadn't been a coffee drinker before, even started drinking coffee during those commutes. Before the morning traffic picked up on the Turnpike, the two of them used their left-over Munchkins for target practice, darting in and out of the toll booths to lob the pastries at each other. I sometimes noticed celebrity athletes and coaches headed to Giants games, and the three of us often laughed together about the weird things we saw, like a prostitute finishing an all-night shift or a couple engaged in oral sex.

We rarely, if ever, missed a day on the Turnpike.

Since we couldn't work during medical school and couldn't call home for cash, there were many days at Rutgers when Rameck and I didn't have money to buy food or the books we needed for class. We had to be creative. One of the things we tried was a scribe service. The business had been handed down to us from a previous medical student. We hired friends for $25 per hour to tape every class and transcribe the notes. We sold the notes to our peers—$125 for all the notes in each of their classes for the entire semester, a real deal. The first semester, Rameck and I made as much as $3,000 each. But our classmates rebelled the next semester and refused to pay for the notes. We never understood their rebellion because the scribe service had been a tradition passed from one graduating class to another. A couple of them tried to start their own service.

Still, we never seemed to have enough to cover our expenses. One class alone required four books. Those were the times when Dr. Hsu stepped in to help. Sometimes we called her when we were in a bind, and she dropped what she was doing to rescue us. She brought us food, books, supplies, whatever we needed. She allowed me to store some of my belongings in her attic during our many moves from dorm to dorm. She invited us to dinner at her home. And she often visited us at Rutgers to make sure we were doing okay. Once, she drove to visit us during a torrential rainstorm and, before leaving, slid $100 into each of our palms, just because.

She knew we were struggling financially, and she constantly assured us that everything would be okay. I tried to believe her. But at home in Newark, things kept getting worse.

During one of my visits home, I had noticed something different about my sister Fellease. She didn't look sick, but the texture of her hair had changed, becoming finer and softer. In the 'hood, that was one of the first visible signs that someone was infected with HIV or AIDS. Fellease and I were always real with each other, so I said something like: "Girl, you got that good hair."

She knew exactly what I meant.

"Boy, I ain't got no HIV," she said.

But later, she told me the truth: she was indeed infected with the virus that causes AIDS. I felt helpless. Here I was, studying to become a doctor, and I could offer nothing to help my own sister.

My mind was always cluttered with worries beyond school, but I kept trying to stay focused. Watching Dr. Hsu go through such trouble to help us inspired me. I didn't want to let her down. I would remember, as Carla Dickson had often told us, that the future of Access Med was linked to our success.

Our senior year came to an end, and we received our final grades: on a scale of Honors, High Pass, Pass, Low Pass, and Fail, I had received High Passes and Passes in all of my classes, and Rameck got a High Pass in each one.

We had succeeded.

Both of us were accepted to Robert Wood Johnson without taking the MCAT. And I clung to the faith that eventually I would find my place in medicine.

# 14

---

## OLD TIES

### *George*

JUST DAYS AFTER GRADUATING from Seton Hall, I packed all of my belongings and moved home to Newark to begin dental school. My mom's apartment in High Park Gardens was practically within walking distance from the University of Medicine and Dentistry of New Jersey downtown. It didn't make much sense to spend money renting an apartment elsewhere when just paying tuition was a struggle.

I moved back into my old room. My mother and I have always been close, so I didn't feel bad asking her if I could move back home. She saw it as just another way to help me. She didn't hassle me too much about the times I stayed out partying, and everything worked out well.

Living so close to campus couldn't have been more convenient. I sometimes zipped home to eat lunch, study, or take a nap during long breaks between classes. But six months after moving home, I faced an unanticipated dilemma. My mother and stepfather got back together and bought a house in Piscataway, the suburb where Sam and Rameck were attending medical school. I could either move to another place or try to maintain the apartment on my own. I decided to keep the apartment because the $340 monthly rent was cheaper than I would find anywhere else. But when Mom tried to turn over her lease to me, the board of directors, all of whom were tenants, resisted. Most of the tenants were older residents who brought stability and security to the complex, and board members didn't want to upset that. But, of course, they didn't tell me that directly. They tried to use my status as a full-time student against me. They said they were concerned that I didn't have a steady income. I explained that my grants and loans would cover the rent. The President of the Board, Blonnie Watson, who had given me my first job as a yard boy at the complex, spoke up for me. Somehow, she persuaded the other board members to give me a chance. I got to keep the apartment.

No one was happier for my mom than I was that she had finally realized her dream of buying a home. She'd been working so hard to help put me through college and dental school that at times I felt guilty. I worried that I was killing her. College and medical school weren't the free ride that Sam, Rameck, and I had expected. The fund that was supposed to cover our tuition had been mismanaged, and we never got the full-tuition scholarship we had been promised. Though university administrators put together packages of grants, loans, and scholarships to cover the bulk of our expenses, we still had to come up with thousands of dollars. Practically every semester, all three of us worried about whether we were going to get kicked out of college over an unpaid tuition bill. My mom got a part-time job. She began her days at seven A.M. at Chubb Insurance, worked until four P.M., and arrived an hour later at Bell Atlantic Mobile, where she worked part-time in the customer-service department for another four hours. Many nights I worried about her driving home alone on deserted highways through the pitch-black swamp after working fourteen-hour days.

Unpaid tuition fees kept accruing each year, and I graduated from Seton Hall with an unpaid balance of more than $6,000. That would cause problems for me during my residency, when the university would go to court, obtain an order, and garnish my checking account for half of the balance at a time when I really couldn't spare it. Because of the unpaid balance, the university also held on to my degree.

When I found myself in a financial jam, I usually waited until the last minute to call my mom. I would try everything else I could think of before turning to her, because I knew she would dip into her retirement savings for me. That is exactly what happened at the end of my senior year of dental school, when it was time to take my state licensing exam. The school passed out literature explaining the logistical details of the exam, but I was so busy preparing for graduation that I forgot to read it until a few days before the test. When my eyes fell on the line about fees of nearly $1,000, I panicked. There was no way I would be able to come up with that amount of money in such a short time. I was too scared to call my mother that night. I lay awake practically all night wondering how I could get the money on my own. Two days before the money was due, I was near tears when I called my mother and asked for her help. She borrowed the money from her 401(k), the fund she had established to secure her future.

Other times, she called on her eight brothers and sisters, who chipped in to help. My mother's friend Deborah and her husband James, a lawyer, also gave me a few hundred dollars a couple of times a year to help buy my books. Deborah had helped put James through law school, so they understood my struggle.

About four months after my mother moved to her new house in Piscataway, I had to call on her for help. Maintaining our old apartment on my own without a job proved to be more difficult than I had anticipated. She told me that I could move in with her and my stepdad in their new home. I packed all of my things, moved to Piscataway, and commuted to school in bumper-to-bumper traffic that stretched a drive that usually took just forty-five minutes into an hour and a half. I couldn't stand it. After just four days, I packed up again and headed back to my apartment in Newark with a new determination to do a better job of budgeting. Fortunately, I had not notified the board or called the utility company about my move, so everything was just as I had left it.

Before I even unpacked, Blonnie Watson called and asked if I wouldn't mind relocating to a one-bedroom apartment so that a new family moving into the complex could have the two-bedroom unit. I agreed and moved two doors down.

I had no idea that living in the old neighborhood again would be such a distraction.

There had been something invigorating and quietly inspiring about the environment at Seton Hall, where I was surrounded daily by thousands of other young men and women all hustling to achieve their dreams. Everywhere you looked, students were huddled in study groups or curled alone on lounge chairs or under trees with their books.

If there was an opposite of that, my neighborhood was it. Sometimes it felt surreal, walking past the drunks, dealers, and addicts on my way home from dental school with a pile of books. I'd wave and greet them with a "Hey, how y'all doing?" and head on up to my apartment. When I tried to study in my room, I'd hear pit-bull fights outside my window or people yelling back and forth across the street. This went on every day, all day.

When I went out, I had to watch my back. The security I felt at Seton Hall had desensitized me to my old environment, causing me to relax too much during my four years in college. One time, the temporary lapse of street smarts could have cost me my life.

One afternoon during my sophomore year at Seton Hall, I drove back to Newark to visit a friend. As I got out of my car, a guy walked up and offered to sell me some brand-new speakers really cheap. I had just bought my car, and I was, like, man, I could use a new sound system.

He asked me to drive him to pick up the speakers. I drove a few blocks, and he showed me where to stop. He got out of the car and began walking toward a more secluded area.

Like a fool, I followed him. All of a sudden, he turned around quickly and pulled out a gun.

"You know what it is," he said.

I gave him $45. He ran away.

I was mad at myself for ignoring the rules of the streets that had kept me alive. But I was madder at the hustler who had just run away with my $45. I hopped in my car and drove to my cousin Reggie's house, not too far away. He was well respected in the streets, and he and my brother were pretty tight. I told Reggie what happened. He was angry. I didn't know it then, but he had told my brother that he would never let anybody mess with me.

"George don't ever mess with nobody," he had told my brother.

He walked into his bedroom, opened the closet, and put something into his jacket. I couldn't see what it was.

"Let's go," he said.

We got in my car and retraced my steps.

"You see him?" my cousin kept asking me, looking for the guy who had just robbed me. "You see him?"

We drove around for fifteen minutes, and I didn't see the guy. But I made a right turn, and there he was. We locked eyes for a second.

"You see him?" my cousin asked again.

"Naw, man," I said. "Let's go home."

Many of the friends who had been like little brothers to me had never even left the neighborhood. They were doing nothing with their lives, or rather, nothing they felt free to talk about. But I was still cool with them. They rang my bell all times of the day and night. I kept an open-door policy because I preferred that they drank a few beers and played video games inside my apartment than that they found trouble in the streets. Sometimes, I drank a beer or two with them. I had started drinking socially in college.

Many of my friends were as deep into the streets as I was into school, but I didn't judge them. When we saw each other, the ten-year-olds we once were came out. They didn't see me as a potential victim of theirs or as a person studying to become a doctor. And I didn't see them as a potential threat. We saw each other as the kids who used to play football together in the parking lot. So they didn't mind leaving their guns behind before walking into my place.

My friends respected me enough not to do certain things in my apartment or in my presence. One time, I overheard one of the guys say to another, "Make sure you don't tell George."

I confronted him.

"Man, you need to leave those streets alone," I said. "If you're even thinking about doing something crazy, you're not plotting it in here."

My apartment was often so full of noisy neighborhood guys that it felt like a boys' club. I learned to tune them out while I was in my bedroom studying. They knew that when I closed my bedroom door, I was studying for a test, and they respected that. They at least kept the noise down to a level that I could block out. It was sort of like living next to a train station. After a while, the noise just blends into the background, and you learn to function in spite of it.

Unfortunately, my neighbors didn't quite see things that

way. I had to appear before the board at least three times to respond to neighbors' complaints about too much noise and traffic in my apartment. I always felt bad about that because I knew that Ms. Watson had vouched for me. One time, her daughter confronted me.

"My mom stuck her neck out for you," she said angrily before giving me a verbal tongue-lashing, no doubt meant to make me feel worse.

I didn't like her coming up to me like that, but she was right. What could I say? I stood there and took it in stride. She couldn't have known how torn I felt between protecting her mother's image and providing a haven for my friends.

I could tell that the whole neighborhood was proud of me. On my way to and from school, men and women in the community stopped to congratulate me or ask if I needed anything. Sometimes, they even knocked on my door to check on me. These were people who had little or nothing themselves, but they were willing to share what they had to help me. Their generosity always reminded me that I was carrying the hopes of a bunch of people when I walked onto that university campus.

Sometimes, though, straddling two distant worlds messed with my head. It felt weird spending the day with my dental-school peers, whose biggest worry was whether they would pass a test, and then returning home to such despair. I was in the middle, and that was a lonely spot. The only people I could relate to during those times were Rameck and Sam. I missed those guys so much.

The three of us had moved into an apartment near cam-

pus together with another guy the summer after our sophomore year at Seton Hall.

At one point Sam, Rameck, and I began to put our money
together to buy one another an inexpensive but thoughtful
birthday gift. Rameck had a busted-up notepad that he used as
a phone book, and Sam and I used to rag on him about it. So
when his birthday rolled around, Sam and I got him a really
nice leather one. Rameck loved that gift. Rameck and I gave
Sam a digital clock because he had an annoying bright orange
wind-up clock that used to crack us up whenever it went off. I
wanted to take a hammer to the old one when we gave Sam
his birthday gift, but he wouldn't allow it.

For my birthday, Rameck and Sam took me to Atlantic
City and gave me money to gamble with. It was sort of a joke
because they always said I had beginner's luck. I always
seemed to win when I tried a new game for the first time. Sure
enough, I won around twenty times that night without losing
a cent. The piece of my winnings that I broke off for each of
them was more than they had given me in the first place. We
all went home a little richer in money and friendship that
night.

When Sam and Rameck moved to New Brunswick to finish their senior year at Rutgers and begin medical school early,
I felt lost. We had been inseparable for all four years of college. Walking to class alone felt weird. But their leaving lit a
fire in me. I had made average grades in college, but I may
have been too comfortable because I knew I could count on
Rameck and Sam to help me study. Sam's tireless work ethic
rubbed off on me. That wasn't one of my natural traits, so I

often wouldn't put the hours and work into studying that he did. But I began to push myself harder because he was my boy. Rameck helped me to develop a more skeptical, analytical side. He taught me to think before accepting what someone says at face value. I tended to give everyone the benefit of the doubt. Rameck was just the opposite. As a result of our friendship, I think I landed somewhere in the middle. Now I would be on my own the rest of the way, and I had to kick my performance up a notch to hold up my end of our deal.

Rameck, Sam, and I always called or visited one another when one of us needed encouragement. In their senior year of college and first year of medical school when they lived in New Brunswick, the drive was about thirty minutes each way. When they moved to South Jersey in the third year to begin clinical rotations, the drive was at least an hour.

I opened up to them about how odd I felt traveling daily between my two worlds. At times those worlds seemed at war, like on the nights I tried to study while sirens blared and yapping pit bulls clawed and mauled each other outside my window.

"Man, I know what you mean," one of them would say.

That meant a lot. Talking to them always helped me put those feelings to bed and focus again on school. School had to be all that mattered if we were to finish.

I was always pretty good at figuring out what to study. The volume of information thrown at you in dental school can be overwhelming, but I was able to home in pretty quickly on what was significant. I could take eighty pages of notes from a lecture and figure out what the professor was going to focus on for a test. I usually picked up clues from the inflection in his voice or the amount of time spent on a subject during a lecture. I'd go over all of my notes a few times but concentrate mostly on the notes I had highlighted. Sometimes that approach backfired, and I got a grade less than I expected. But 80 percent of the time, I got that B+.

When it was time to study for the first state board exam at the end of my second year, I always wore cargo pants with lots of pockets. I transferred my notes to index cards and stuffed the cards in all of my pockets. Whenever I had a moment of down time, whether I was at a party or riding in the car with a friend, I pulled out my cards to study.

But no matter how hard I tried to focus on school, home competed for my attention. Soon after I moved back to Newark, I heard that my childhood friend, Na-im, was sleeping on another friend's couch every night. I went over to see him and invited him to stay with me until he could get himself together. At the time, I was still living in the two-bedroom apartment.

Na-im and I had first met as kids living in the Stella Wright Housing Projects. He was three years younger, but he and I were in the same gifted-and-talented program at Louise A. Spencer Elementary. His situation at home wasn't as stable as mine, though, and he later started selling drugs to take care of himself and his younger brother. Then he dropped out of high school. I was away at college when he, at the age of sixteen, got busted for selling drugs. He didn't serve any time in jail, but he was sentenced to home detention and wore an ankle monitor for a few months. The arrest was enough to turn him away from his former trade, but he seemed unable to snap the pieces of his life into place afterward. I respected him because he was determined not to go back to selling drugs, even if it meant being unsure every night where he would lay his head. I wanted to help him.

"Look, man, I've got an extra bedroom," I told him. "You can stay there. Don't worry about anything. I've got the same bills whether you're in my apartment or not."

When I moved to the one-bedroom apartment, Na-im slept on my sofa. My only rule was that he had to be out looking for a job, going to school, or doing something productive every day. He couldn't just lie around my apartment doing nothing. I always pushed him. I bought him books to study for his high-school equivalency diploma and took him to Essex County College to find out the dates when the test would be given. But it was extremely difficult to motivate him. He was completely drained of hope.

About two and a half years after Na-im moved in, he confided in me that he was worried about his seventeen-year-old brother, Abdul, who lived in Irvington with an aunt. Abdul, a junior in high school, had begun skipping classes and hanging with the wrong crowd. I was worried that Abdul would repeat his brother's mistake, so I invited him to move in with us. I thought I might be able to talk some sense into him. Every day, I talked to him and pushed him to go to school.

"Man, you see how hard a time Na-im is having," I told him. "As long as you have a plan, I'll help you."

Abdul stayed with me about six months, and Na-im stayed

more than three years. But in my last year of dental school, just months before I graduated, my brother Garland moved back to Newark from Atlanta, where he had spent the past eight years. He needed a place to stay and didn't want to move to the suburbs with our parents. He moved in with me, too. That meant four guys were now sharing a one-bedroom apartment. None of the others was working, so I was carrying everybody's weight.

My big brother is a good guy, but he and I are total opposites. As a kid, Garland hated school and brought home F's all the time. When he was in high school, he once brought home a report card showing a vast improvement in his grades. He had four B's, three C's, and a D. Our mom, who rarely gets excited about anything, was thrilled. She had this look of relief on her face that said she was finally getting through to him. But when she held the report card up to the light, she realized it was a big hoax. All of the grades had been changed with a typewriter. Garland had failed practically every class. I never forgot the disappointment on my mom's face. I never wanted to make her feel that way.

The month after my brother moved in, my telephone bill arrived with more than $300 in long-distance charges, and nobody owned up to them. Though I had my suspicions, I couldn't prove who had done it. I knew then that it was time to clean house. I asked all three of them to leave. I had helped them as much as I could. Graduation from dental school was months away, and I needed to focus on my future.

Na-im eventually got a job, bought himself a car, and

began studying again for his high-school equivalency diploma. Sometimes we went together to the public library to study. But despite my best efforts, Abdul still dropped out of high school. That was a huge disappointment. Having grown up without a father for much of my life, I knew the importance of male role models. I had been fortunate to know good men, including my friends, who stood in the gap and taught me life lessons, large and small.

It was Rameck, for example, who helped me choose my first car and taught me how to drive it.

I was a sophomore at Seton Hall and needed a car to get back and forth to work and school. My mom gave me about $3,000 to buy a used car, and I wanted to get a good deal. Rameck had just bought his second car, the white Volkswagen Golf, so he volunteered to walk me through the process. He took me to a small car dealership and introduced me to the salesman who had sold him his car. We spent a couple of hours checking out the cars on the lot before settling on a gray, two-door 1986 Volkswagen Jetta. It didn't have power steering or air conditioning, and only the front windows rolled up and down. But it had a great engine and was within my price range.

There was one major drawback: it had a standard transmission, and I didn't know how to drive a stick shift. Rameck assured me that he could teach me. For two days, my car sat idle in the parking lot at Seton Hall. I grew frustrated. One morning about one A.M., I walked across the hall and banged on Rameck's door. He had been out partying and was in no condition to drive.

"Ra, man, I know you been out and everything, but I need to learn how to drive my car right now," I said.

I knew the basics. I just needed some practice. Without saying a word, Rameck got up and followed me to the parking lot. I got behind the wheel and slipped the car into gear, but I released the clutch too quickly and it stalled. After a few tries, I bucked out of the parking lot and down the main street leading off campus. I picked up speed, but when I tried to change gears, the car again jerked to a stop in the middle of the street. A car traveling behind me slammed on its brakes and skidded into the back of my car. Fortunately, the Jetta was so sturdy that it didn't even get a scratch, so I let the driver go without exchanging telephone numbers. When I hopped back into the driver's seat, Rameck burst out laughing. We laughed all the way back to Seton Hall.

Someone always seemed to be there when I needed fatherly advice or instructions. One time was in the second year of dental school and the first day of class with a conservative professor named Dr. Nicholas. I had heard rumors that he made all of the guys wear ties to class. I had managed to complete the first year of dental school without even wearing dress shoes, let alone a tie.

When Dr. Nicholas made the announcement, I started to sweat. No one had ever taught me how to knot a tie. Throughout high school, I had avoided wearing one or someone had tied it for me on the spot. The next morning, I dug through the drawers in my apartment until I found an old, multicolored silk tie. I clasped it tightly and dashed to class.

I got there a few minutes early and stood at the door. My

eyes worked the room and landed on Jason Karns, a classmate with a kind face and a perfectly knotted tie. I walked up to him.

"Look, uh, I need this tie tied," I said.

Jason must have seen the embarrassment in my eyes. He could have tied it for me right then and there, as I expected him to do. Without saying a word, he motioned for me to follow him down the hall to the bathroom. He took my tie and showed me step by step how to knot it. He took it apart and retied it slowly two or three times. Then, I took it apart and practiced two or three more times.

I tied it one last time.

And from that moment on, the knot I wore was my own.

# 15

## D.W.B.

### *Rameck*

*November 10, 1996, about 2 A.M.*

I noticed the three cop cars just blocks down the road behind me. I had gotten together with friends to watch the Mike Tyson–Evander Holyfield fight and ended up staying late to socialize after Holyfield shocked boxing fans everywhere with a TKO of Tyson just seconds into the eleventh round.

That many police in one place meant something was going on. It was a rainy night; I rolled down my window to get a better look. The officers were laughing. Maybe they had watched the fight, too. I locked eyes with one of them for a second. The laughter stopped. I glanced at my friend Dax, who was riding in the front seat.

"Man, you know they're about to follow us," he said.

All three officers jumped in their cars and fell in behind us, single file.

We knew the drill. Practically every black man who has ever been behind the wheel of a car knows the drill: make sure you're not speeding. Use the proper turn signals. Double-check your seat belt. Double-check your lights. Don't make one wrong move.

Without clicking on their red lights or sirens, they followed every turn I made for the next ten minutes, just waiting for me to slip.

"Man, why are they following us?" Dax asked, though he already knew the answer.

I was taking my normal route home and turned onto a dark, secluded street. Seconds later, red lights began flashing in my rear-view mirror. The steering wheel dampened in my grip. The warnings I had heard about Edison cops when I first learned to drive came rushing back: be careful there. They don't like black folks.

I began to second-guess myself. Maybe I shouldn't have made that turn. Who knows what three crazy white cops might do to two young, black men on a dark street in a predominantly white suburb this time of the morning? It didn't matter that I was a first-year medical student or that Dax was in law school. The color of our skin alone was enough to make us suspect.

This was three years before the state of New Jersey signed a consent decree, agreeing to a major overhaul of its state police to end racial profiling and avoid a civil-rights lawsuit by the U.S. Department of Justice—a case that helped to catapult the term "racial profiling" onto the front pages of newspapers across the nation. On this night, racial profiling—the crime of driving while black—was just a truth shared among black men.

I was approaching a green traffic light. I rolled through, veered right, and began to pull to the side of the road. At the same time, the officer in the last car sped around the others, made a quick turn in front of me, and cut me off.

He jumped out of the car with his gun drawn. The cop in the car immediately behind me clicked on his floodlights and jumped out of his car, too.

"Get the fuck out of the car," the cop with the gun yelled.

Startled, Dax and I looked at each other. My knees felt weak as I stepped slowly out of the car. The officer ordered Dax out, too. I was sure we were about to die.

One of the officers rushed over and slammed me against my car.

"Didn't you see my lights?" he yelled.

He pointed his finger in my face so close that it was almost touching.

"Why in the fuck didn't you stop?"

"I did stop," I said.

"Not fast enough," he shouted back.

He began patting me.

"Why are you frisking me?" I asked. "What's going on?"

"Shut the fuck up," the officer said. "You should have pulled over when you saw our lights."

The other officers started looking through my car.

"Hey, man, you can't go through my car," I said. "Why are you searching my car?"

They ignored me and popped my trunk.

"You got any drugs or guns?" they asked, continuing their search without waiting for me to answer.

"Aha! Look what I found," one of the officers yelled gleefully from inside the car.

I shook my head in disbelief.

Oh, my God, what have they planted inside my car? I wondered.

The officer held up a small knife about the size of a pencil. It was an old fishing knife that I had thrown into the glove compartment and forgotten. It never occurred to me that carrying it around was illegal.

"You're being a smart-ass. Now you're going to jail," the officer said.

He snapped on a pair of handcuffs, much too tightly, and left me standing in the rain while he stepped away to talk to his fellow officers. Within minutes, I was soaked. I was grateful for the heavier-than-usual traffic because I figured it offered a bit more protection. But at the same time, I was deeply embarrassed. Passengers stared as cars slowed almost to a stop. I looked up in time to see one guy in a passing car shake his head at me in disgust. Finally, the officer led me to a police car and pushed me into the backseat.

"It ain't no black thing either," he said. "You should have pulled over when we told you to."

"Man, I'm a medical student. My friend is about to go to law school. You're not taking me anywhere until you call your supervisor," I said.

He called for a sergeant over the car radio. At least three more police cars rolled up. An officer I presumed was a sergeant was in one of them. He walked over to the car where I was and listened as the officers told their side of the story. He walked away without even acknowledging me.

I noticed a couple of officers talking to Dax, who was still standing next to my car. They allowed him to drive my car home. But they took me to jail and booked me with some ridiculous charges: interference with a police officer and possession of a deadly weapon. They put me in a cell alone.

I couldn't believe this was happening. I hadn't done anything wrong. And possession of a deadly weapon is a felony—I would never pass the medical-licensing process with a felony on my record as an adult. I would never become a doctor now.

I looked up to find a white officer I hadn't seen before standing outside my cell. He identified himself as a sergeant.

"How you doing?" he asked. His voice was kind.

"I'm all right," I said calmly.

"What happened?"

For the first time, I told my side of the story. He glanced to his right, then his left, as though he was looking for someone. No one was there.

"You should file a complaint," he said, then walked away.

About three hours after I was locked up, an officer unlocked the cell.

"Your friends are upstairs," he said when I asked to use the phone.

I have never been so happy to see George, Sam, Dax, and Na-im. When the officers let Dax go, he had driven to our apartment and picked up Sam. They called George, who told them he and Na-im would meet them at the Edison jail. All four of them had been waiting for hours.

When I made it home, it was nearly seven A.M. I couldn't sleep. I sat alone in my room and replayed the night's events in my head. A few hours later, I called my mother and told her what had happened. She promised to call her lawyer, who had gotten her out of trouble a few times before. The lawyer agreed to represent me pro bono as a favor to my mother. I explained that I was not open to a plea bargain. My career would have to survive this, and the only way was to get the charges wiped off my record.

My lawyer advised me that the simplest approach would be to persuade the officer to drop the charges. He assured me that he would take care of it. In the meantime, I went back to the police station and filed a complaint.

As the weeks passed, I had trouble sleeping. A couple of times, bad dreams jolted me awake in a cold sweat. I had worked so hard to change my life. Now I could lose everything.

During a preliminary hearing, I saw the arrest report for the first time, which explained why the officers claimed they had stopped me. The tint on my windows and dirty license-plate cover made me look suspicious, they said. Before the hearing began, my lawyer walked over to the prosecutor, sat next to him, and began to whisper. He pleaded my case and asked the prosecutor, a young guy fresh out of law school, to persuade the police officer to drop the charges. The prosecutor seemed to sympathize and agreed to help. Both lawyers then asked the judge to postpone the hearing.

When I heard from my lawyer again, the news was bad. The officer had refused to drop the charges. The prosecutor suspected that the reason was because I had filed a complaint against the officer. The complaint had been reviewed and resolved in his favor, but it still went in his personnel file as a complaint.

The judge set a trial date. But on the day the judge was scheduled to hear my case, my attorney didn't show up. The judge set a new date. My lawyer missed it again. The judge set a third date. My lawyer missed that one, too.

The judge was angry.

"Listen, young man," he said to me, "I don't know who your lawyer is, but he has no respect for you or your well-being. I'm about to set a new date, and this case will be tried with or without your lawyer. If I were you, I would sue him and get a new lawyer."

By now, I was frantic. While my peers planned their futures and anticipated clinical rotations at hospitals in the area for the following semester, I was worrying that this might be the end for me.

I had no money and no way of getting a new lawyer, and I feared a public defender would try to plead my life away. I turned to Dr. Tiedrich, a Jewish physician who had become my friend while treating my mother for a job-related injury. When she had bragged to him that her son was in medical school, he had asked to meet me. She had persuaded me to accompany her to his office. I did, and he became something of a mentor. He called regularly.

During one of those calls, I explained what was going on.

He called an attorney who was a friend of his. His friend agreed to help. When the new trial date rolled around, my new lawyer and I showed up in court without a clue about what kind of defense to use. The knife found in my car was indeed mine, and under the circumstances, it was against the law.

"God, please help me out of this," I prayed silently.

The judge called my case. My attorney and I sat behind a table on one side of the courtroom. I looked into the audience and saw the police officer again for the first time since my arrest. The charges were read. The prosecutor approached the judge, who hastily called a recess. I wondered what was going on.

After a brief recess, the trial began again.

"Well, we can't seem to find the evidence," the prosecutor said.

I couldn't believe it. They had lost the knife.

The prosecutor asked the judge to postpone the trial again. Clearly frustrated, the judge refused. Instead, he threw the case out.

My mouth dropped open. God had rescued me once again.

And I was free to go.

# 16

# BECOMING DOCTORS

## *Sam*

MY STOMACH TWISTED into a pretzel as I waited to meet with the medical-school dean to learn the results of my first state board exam.

All medical students take the exam at the end of their second year, and the results determine whether they can move on to the next phase, working eight-week rotations in different areas of medicine at hospitals affiliated with the university. The results hadn't arrived by the beginning of the next semester, so Rameck and I had moved to Camden and started our clinical rotations at Cooper Hospital, adjacent to the South Jersey branch of Robert Wood Johnson. Dr. Paul R. Mehne, Associate Dean for Academic and Student Affairs at the branch, had received the results first and made appointments with each of us to break the news.

He didn't waste any time.

"We didn't make it," he said sympathetically.

His words knocked the wind out of me.

"But it's not a problem," he continued, quickly trying to make it better. "We're going to get you past this. I guarantee you you'll be fine."

I had missed the mark by just a couple of points. But that didn't matter. For a few seconds, I couldn't breathe. I couldn't speak. I couldn't see how I would ever get past this.

I had used review books and practice tests and had regularly stayed up studying all night. Everything I had worked for the past six years had come down to this one exam. The night before, I had been unable to sleep. On test day, I had trouble concentrating. Exhaustion had shut down my brain like a computer virus, scrambling or wiping out everything I had learned. When I'd walked out of the classroom after finishing, I knew I had failed.

I had just been hoping I was wrong.

Dr. Mehne was genuinely warm and encouraging as he broke the news. He still believed in me, he said. But I had to suspend my clinical rotations for six weeks to prepare to retake the exam.

When I walked into my apartment that evening, Camille, who had moved in with Rameck and me when we relocated to Camden, was standing in the kitchen. When she saw my face, she knew something was wrong.

I told her I didn't make it.

She rushed over, embraced me, and began to cry. I was still too stunned to cry. Rameck came out of his bedroom and joined us. He knew immediately what was going on.

"Aw, dog, I'm so sorry," he said. "But don't worry, it's gonna be all right."

They had met with Dr. Mehne, too. They didn't even have to tell me they had passed.

When I told George about my results over the telephone that evening, he drove all the way from Newark just to sit with me. Guys don't like to make each other uncomfortable, so we didn't really talk about it. He just wanted to be there.

The three of us had always been successful together, so this was awkward for us. Neither of them knew what to say to me. The truth is, there was nothing much they could say to make it better. I had to get through this on my own.

"Whenever you need me, dog, I'm here," Rameck told me constantly.

In college, he and I had always talked through our problems or shared what we were going through during long conversations at night. But this was different. I needed all of my energy just to survive each day. I felt like a complete failure, like a boxer who had gotten knocked out in the first round of an important fight by an intimidating opponent he had to face again in just a few weeks.

Medical school had not been a nurturing, supportive environment, and from the beginning I had felt that I didn't belong. Failing the board exam only heightened my sense of isolation. I had no confidence in myself. There was no joy in waking up each morning. As close as Rameck, George, and I were, I wasn't sure even they could relate.

George called regularly and occasionally drove to Camden to check on me, and Rameck and I still played basketball together. But there were long periods of silence when we got together. For whatever reasons, my two best friends weren't able to reach me.

Camille was the one who broke through. She had struggled in her first two years of medical school and knew exactly what I was feeling. I had been her backbone during that difficult time, and she became mine. We often hung out, just to talk. She became my sister. We were able to connect on an emotional level that feels too awkward between guys.

"You might not understand it now," she said. "But God allowed this to happen for a reason."

Alone in my room, I listened to Tupac. He rapped about the pull between his old life as a thug and the new one as a rich rapper. I related to his isolation.

But as defeated as I felt, I never stopped pushing myself. Every morning, I got up early, as though I was still going to the hospital. Instead, I went to the library. I studied review books in every subject, including surgery, anatomy, microbiology, cell biology/histology, and physiology. Periodically, I tested myself with practice questions. Sometimes I teamed up with a fellow student named Terry Rollins, a super-smart guy from Atlantic City, to go over questions and concepts. I brought my lunch and took a scheduled break to eat.

In the evenings, I studied with two girls who had also failed. We had hung together before at school, and now we bonded and worked to help one another through. They were roommates, so their apartment became our study hall. They often cooked dinner, and I went jogging through their complex listening to Tupac's "Me Against the World" and "Makaveli."

Then we spread our books across the table or floor and spent the rest of the night studying. To lighten the moment, we told stories to make each other laugh. God knows I needed to laugh.

I also traveled to Washington, D.C., to hang out with our former roommate, Dax, who was attending law school at George Washington University. The change of scenery was refreshing.

One of the best things I did for myself was to seek counseling from advisers I had come to trust, mainly Carla Dickson and Geoffrey Young, Assistant Dean of Student Affairs on the Piscataway campus of Robert Wood Johnson. I didn't tell Rameck or George.

I needed to understand why I had failed and what I was supposed to learn from it. I also sought to understand my purpose in medicine. I had reached that point in life where I asked: What is my purpose? What role do I play? Where do I belong?

My counselors suggested that I find a way to relieve some of the stress. I began meditating each morning the way Reggie had taught me during kung fu lessons a decade earlier, and I worked out during my lunch break. I came to understand that I had defeated myself mentally even before I took the exam. In my mind, the exam had become insurmountable.

I had to change my thoughts.

During meditation, I reminded myself that I was smart enough to pass this exam, and I tried to regain my inner peace. I focused on clearing my mind, just relaxing and focusing on the rewards that life had brought me thus far. I wasn't happy, but I had to make the best of the situation.

When test time rolled around again, I went to bed early the night before. On the morning of the test, I tried to stay calm.

"I can do this," I kept repeating in my head.

Answers to the test questions flowed more freely. Before I was even halfway done, I knew I would pass.

When I went to Dr. Mehne's office to get the results this time, his smile told me what I wanted to hear: I had passed.

Thank God, I could move on.

I resumed my clinical rotations, but the feeling of sheer elation didn't last long. I continued to feel out of place, especially when my peers talked about the invitations they received to play golf with residents at the hospital or to have dinner at the home of the head doctor. I was never included.

But no matter how uncertain I felt about becoming a doctor, I knew that returning home to my old life was not an option. Seeing an old friend again one day reminded me of that.

It was summertime, and I was visiting my mother at home. Whenever my old friends saw my car parked outside, they would stand in front of my house underneath my bedroom window and yell, "Yo, Marshall," until I came out. Every day, I walked over to the projects to visit Will, Noody, and my other friends. There one day I encountered one of the guys who had participated with me in the robbery. At fifteen, he had been the youngest in the group. When I saw him again, he was in his early twenties and had just been released from jail after serving time for another crime.

We hugged each other the way guys do.

"Man, I ain't seen you in a long time," he began. "You don't stay down here no more, huh?"

"Naw, man, I just been doing this school thing," I said.

"How long you did?" he asked.

He figured I was still out there banging and had spent some time in jail. In our neighborhood, you don't just walk away from the streets. You keep hustling until you either get too old or too sick, or until you get knocked.

"C'mon man, that ain't me," I responded, trying to be vague.

Staying vague kept them guessing and protected you.

"Well, hey, don't get caught out here. Let's get together and catch up."

"Cool," I said.

He wished me well, and we parted ways. We never got together, and I knew we never would. I had become a different person. Seeing my old friend again reminded me of just how much my life had changed.

I spent my third year working eight-week rotations in pediatrics, surgery, psychiatry, internal medicine, family practice, and obstetrics/gynecology at Cooper Hospital. As students, we mostly shadowed residents, and the head doctor lectured us once a week.

I made High Passes in most of my courses in my third year and passed the second state board exam the following summer with no problems. My academic performance was just as good in my fourth year.

During the fourth year, each medical student got to choose an area of specialty and work a rotation either at Cooper Hospital, which is next to the Camden branch of the medical school, or out of town. I decided to give it a go at another hospital. The six disciplines I had studied in my third year had not intrigued me, but I wanted to try emergency medicine. I chose Hahnemann Medical College of Philadelphia. I had heard that it had a good training program in the field, and I figured I could gather the practical experience to determine whether I wanted to pursue emergency medicine.

I drove forty minutes each way daily for two weeks that summer to a small community hospital affiliated with the university. The head doctor, Dr. Carol Hart, made me feel like part of the emergency-room team, as we evaluated patients and determined the appropriate treatments. This was the first time in all four years of medical school that something had felt right to me.

Rameck and I decided to go together to Atlanta to explore the program at Emory University. One of our friends, Jerry Filmore, had done a rotation the year before and was now a first-year resident in emergency medicine. The two of us were stationed for four weeks at Grady Hospital, a large medical center that serves mostly city-dwellers. We stayed in an apartment building owned by the hospital. I worked in the emergency room, and Rameck worked in gastrointestinal medicine. The size of the hospital alone was intimidating, but I caught on to the fast-paced rhythm pretty quickly. I liked the variety of problems we treated—from simple muscle strains to heart attacks; from minor lacerations to gunshot wounds. The work required an ability to think quickly in developing strategies for medical treatments and interventions, and I excelled at that. I've always been good working with my hands. This was what I had been waiting for.

When the time came to apply for a residency, I decided to pursue emergency medicine. But I started the process late because I was still trying to decide whether that was truly what I wanted to do. About 16,000 medical students throughout the country apply for residencies each year through the Washington, D.C.–based National Resident Matching Program, which uses a computerized database to match students with teaching hospitals. Students do research to find hospitals with their specialties, apply for those positions, and then rank their top choices in the computerized database. In the end, the hospitals list their student choices in the database, and the computer sorts the matches. During an annual event called Match Day, medical students throughout the country learn simultaneously where they will spend the next years as a resident.

An Internet Web site helped me identify the hospitals that had slots in emergency medicine, and I applied to about forty of them. I was invited for interviews at hospitals in New York, Chicago, Baltimore, Atlanta, and Cleveland and spent at least $2,000 traveling to those cities.

But I didn't realize that emergency medicine was so competitive.

Two days before Match Day, the dean called me into his office for more bad news: I had not matched in emergency medicine. None of my top choices of hospitals had listed me among their top choices of students. The dean gave me a list of hospitals that still had residency positions available in various disciplines. Most of my classmates had matched at hospitals on their lists and would find out on Match Day where they would be going. But along with other students who had not matched, I spent an entire day on the telephone scrambling to find a position.

I knew Rameck had listed the University of Maryland as his first or second choice and Robert Wood Johnson Hospital as the other. He had kept changing the order of his top two picks until the deadline arrived for submitting our lists. The University of Maryland still had a residency slot available, but the position was in internal medicine. I called, and the resident coordinator asked me to submit my application via the computer. The program there was reputable, but I had no interest in internal medicine. Time was running out, though. If I didn't find a slot, I would have to wait another year to reapply.

The day before Match Day, I was offered the slot at the University of Maryland.

Just before noon on March 18, 1999, I met with my peers in a lecture hall at the hospital for the Match Day ceremony. Dozens of bottles of champagne were lined up across the stage. Each student was handed a sealed envelope bearing the code that the computer had used to match us. At exactly noon, the dean instructed us to open our envelopes. Medical students across the country were opening their envelopes at the same time.

Rameck and I ripped open our envelopes. He had matched at his top choice, Robert Wood Johnson Hospital. I was happy for him, but disappointed. I already knew what was inside my envelope. Since Rameck wouldn't be going to the University of Maryland, I would have to go there alone.

The room quickly filled with shrieks of excitement. My peers hugged one another and rushed around the room to find out where their colleagues had matched. I stood back and observed quietly. I was in no mood to celebrate. I again felt disappointed. I had no idea—and still don't—why I hadn't matched in emergency medicine. I had the grades. Maybe I had begun the process too late, or maybe it was my lack of comfort during interviews at the hospitals. All I knew was that the match process, like everything else in medical school, had come as a surprise.

I had heard about it for the first time just before it was time for me to go through it. No one had ever sat me down and explained step by step what to expect in medical school. I was always finding out about courses and events the day of the deadline or just days before, which left little time to develop a strategy for success or even to prepare myself mentally.

I signed a letter of intent, committing myself as a resident at the University of Maryland. I knew immediately that I had made a big mistake.

I was tired of fighting.

I couldn't understand why everything had been such a struggle for me. I told myself that I had fulfilled the pact. I had finished college and was near completing medical school with George and Rameck. But graduation would be the end of this road for me. I had never promised my friends that I would actually practice medicine. Maybe I would be happier doing something else. After trying so hard and giving so much, I at least deserved to be happy.

Business still interested me, so I thought that perhaps I could use my medical background to find a position with a medical insurance company or health maintenance organization. I also considered enrolling in business school to earn an MBA. I called the Wharton School of Business in Philadelphia and requested an application. I wasn't sure how George and Rameck would react, so I decided not to tell them right away.

I did, however, tell a friend from college named Patrick, who lived in South Jersey, and he said that his mother—the chief executive officer of a drug rehabilitation center in Atlantic City—might be able to help. I called her, and she promised to put me in touch with the head of a Preferred Physicians Organization there. The next time I talked to her, she had arranged an interview for me in Atlantic City.

I drove forty-five minutes to Atlantic City, and the two of us had lunch with the PPO executive. It didn't take them long to figure out that I was suffering from burnout. The executive showed me around his company, but both he and my friend's mother tried to encourage me to go ahead with my residency. They said it would be a mistake to quit before getting a feel for what medicine was really like.

I spent one day in Atlantic City. Before I left, the executive offered me a job as a billing manager making about $30,000 a year, a position I think he knew that I would turn down. Still, I wasn't persuaded to take a residency that I did not want.

In April, just weeks before graduation, I called Carla Dickson.

I met her at a restaurant in South Orange for lunch one spring afternoon. After lunch, we went to a park and sat on a bench to talk. She knew what I had gone through in medical school. This was it, I told her. I was done with medicine. The sadness in my eyes told her that I was serious. For the first time, she didn't have an answer.

After a few seconds, she said: "If you don't want to go to the University of Maryland, just call the representative and tell her you're not coming."

"But is that the right thing to do?" I asked.

I was afraid to back out of the University of Maryland position because I had signed the letter of intent. The match process is practically as binding as the NBA draft. It was almost unheard of to back out of a match after signing a letter of intent. When I had complained about not wanting to go, my professors and colleagues had warned me not to change my mind. It could wreck my career, they said. And further, I could be held legally liable.

But what Carla said next brought clarity.

"This is your life, Sam," she said. "You have to do what's best for Sam. What does Sam really want to do?"

I knew then I was not going to take the slot in Maryland.

But there was still a part of me that didn't want to give up on emergency medicine, a part of me that didn't want to be defeated. The next week, I decided to search the Internet to find out how many emergency-medicine programs there were in New Jersey. I was shocked by what I found. Beth Israel Hospital in Newark had a program in emergency medicine. The hospital hadn't been listed among the programs I'd found when I did my initial computer search before the match process. The computer was now showing that all of the hospital's resident positions had been filled. I decided to take a long shot and call the hospital anyway.

I took a deep breath, picked up the telephone, and called Jacquie Johnson, the resident coordinator there. I hit the lottery. She said the hospital had expanded its residency slots that year and had not filled all of them. She asked me to send my application. A few days later, I was invited to the hospital for an interview.

I can't describe how comfortable I felt when I walked through those doors. I felt immediately that I was home; that I was where I belonged. I reminded myself to stay calm and answer the interview questions from my heart. I felt surprisingly at ease and connected to the doctors interviewing me. When the interview was finished, I knew things had gone well.

I was invited for a second interview. Then the resident director called and offered me the slot. I wanted to accept right away, but first I had to notify the University of Maryland that I wouldn't be coming. I still anguished over making that telephone call and had kept putting it off.

Finally, I called. I explained that my heart was set on working in emergency medicine and that I would not be happy there. I shared how difficult the decision to back out of the agreement had been for me. When I finished talking, I expected the worst, maybe even the threat of a lawsuit. Instead, the woman on the other end was understanding. She said the university didn't want me there if I wouldn't be happy, and she wished me well.

The fear and frustration I had felt for weeks slid off my shoulders. Something mystical—I believe the power of God—was at work here. I was about to return as a doctor to the same hospital where I was born.

I was going back home.

## Sam on

# PERSEVERANCE

Medical school was one of the roughest periods of my life. Something unexpected was always threatening to knock me out of the game: family distractions, the results of my first state board exam, the outcome of my initial search for a residency. But through determination, discipline, and dedication, I was able to persevere.

I call them my three D's, and I believe that they are the perfect formula for survival, no matter what you are going through.

Determination is simply fixing your mind on a desired outcome, and I believe it is the first step to a successful end in practically any situation. When I made the pact with George and Rameck at the age of seventeen, I was desperate to change my life. Going to college and medical school with my friends seemed the best way to make that happen.

But, of course, I had no idea of the challenges awaiting me, and many times over the years I felt like giving up. Trust me, even if you're the most dedicated person, you can get weary when setbacks halt or interfere with your progress. But determination means nothing without the discipline to go through the steps necessary to reach your goal—whether you're trying to lose weight or finish college—and the dedication to stick with it.

When I failed the state board exam, the light in the tunnel disappeared. But I just kept crawling toward my goal. I sought counseling when I needed it, and I found at least one person with whom I could share the range of emotions I was experiencing. If you're going through a difficult time and can't see your way out alone, you should consider asking for help. I know how difficult that is for most guys. We're raised to believe that it's a sign of weakness even to display emotions, let alone ask for help. But reaching out to counselors I had come to trust over the years and talking to my roommate Camille helped me unload some of the weight I was carrying. Only then was I able to focus clearly on what I needed to do to change my circumstances.

I'm grateful that I took kung fu lessons as a kid, because the discipline I learned back then really helped me to stay consistent once I started meditating, working out, and studying every single day. It wasn't easy, but those were the steps required to get where I wanted to be. Concentrating on getting through each day kept me from feeling overwhelmed. And reflection helped me to see that I had overcome tremendous barriers. In the beginning, during a trying adolescence, I'd felt like I was a good kid caught up in a bad situation and truly had to work diligently to overcome obstacles. You can't choose the circumstances that you're born in. However, you can use your insight and hunger to push forward. Life's challenges helped me to maintain my focus and remain humble.

Family matters—my brother's injury, my sister's diagnosis, my mother's financial struggles back home—sometimes competed for my full attention. There is no one-size-fits-all way to handle family issues. Everybody's family and circumstances are different. But I realized that to remain focused on my goal I couldn't focus so much on my family, especially when the energy I expended worrying about them didn't change a thing.

Another important ingredient of perseverance is surrounding yourself with friends who support your endeavor. I can't tell you how much it helped me to have George and Rameck in my life to help me reach my goal. Even though things were awkward between us for a while after I failed the state boards, just knowing they were there and that they expected me to succeed motivated me.

I found motivation wherever I could. One of my college professors once told me that I didn't have what it takes to be a doctor, and I even used that to motivate me. I love being the underdog. I love it when someone expects me to fail. That, like nothing else, can ignite my three D's.

And when success comes, I'm the one who's not surprised.

My motto is simply: no one can tell me that I can't succeed. I've come to believe that every goal in life is obtainable and that the only limitations are the ones you set for yourself. For some, the road to success is merely based on taking advantage of opportunities provided to them. For others, the road is much more difficult because they have to create opportunities for themselves. When you have to find a way where there seems to be none, as I sometimes had to do, success in the end is even sweeter.

I had to keep getting up when life knocked me down. There is nothing sweeter than stealing victory from the jaws of defeat. The closest I ever came to giving up was when I didn't match at any of the hospitals I had listed. But again, something on the inside wouldn't let me quit. And my last try, on the Internet, brought amazing results.

That's how life is sometimes. When you've failed repeatedly and think you're done, that last try—the one that requires every ounce of will and strength you have—is often the one to pull you through.

# 17

## GRADUATION

*George*

FOR A WHILE, it seemed that both Sam and I would land in Maryland for our residencies. I was considering joining the U.S. Air Force as a dentist, and I expected to be stationed at Andrews Air Force Base, about an hour down the road from Baltimore. The Air Force was offering a $30,000 one-time signing bonus, not including salary and benefits, to entice recruits to its medical corps. The money caught my attention.

An Air Force van picked up several classmates and me and drove us to Maryland to tour Andrews in our senior year of dental school. We walked through Air Force Two, the vice president's plane, and saw Air Force One, the president's plane, up close. But I changed my mind about joining the military. I had just spent a grueling eight years in college and dental school, and I realized that I didn't want to face the rigors of boot camp or the everyday restrictions of military life.

I could have graduated from dental school and gone to work right away as a dentist. A dentist isn't required to do a residency. But I figured a residency would give me the practical experience I needed and make me more competitive. I learned that there was an opening in dentistry for a general-practice resident at the University of Medicine and Dentistry of New Jersey in Newark, the same place that had first inspired my dream to become a dentist. I talked to Zia Shey, Associate Dean of the Dental School, and expressed an interest. I interviewed and was offered the position. About the same time, Sam and Rameck told me they had accepted residencies in the Newark area—Sam at Beth Israel Medical Center and Rameck at Robert Wood Johnson.

We would end up at home together.

It had never occurred to me that our graduation ceremonies would be at the same time. One day, near the end of my last semester in dental school, I asked them the dates and places of their graduations. When they told me that their ceremonies were set for May 26 at the PNC Bank Arts Center in Holmdel, I realized that there would be one ceremony for the entire University of Medicine and Dentistry of New Jersey system. We would graduate together.

Rameck and I decided to invite some of our favorite teachers and counselors from University High School to our graduation. One of the staff members we invited was Dr. Valerie Noble, a guidance counselor who had encouraged us in high school. We often went to our guidance counselors when we needed to talk about a personal problem or had career questions, and they were always helpful. Dr. Noble was extremely proud that Rameck, Sam, and I had remained friends and were now about to graduate from medical school. Knowing our backgrounds, she said she couldn't stop thinking about what an extraordinary accomplishment we had achieved. In the days before graduation, she told a reporter she knew about us.

When Dr. Noble called and told us that the local paper was interested in writing a story about us, I was more puzzled than excited. I didn't understand what the big deal was—hundreds of students were graduating from medical school that day—but we agreed to be interviewed. We met with the reporter before graduation.

It was a beautiful, sunny morning, and we arrived in our black caps and gowns and colorful hoods. My mother, my father, my grandmother, and most of my aunts and uncles, as well as my childhood friends—Na-im and Abdul, Shahid Jackson and his father and brother—were all there. When I saw my aunt Lestine Graves, I was reminded how much her achievements had inspired me. Aunt Lestine had been in her early forties when she returned to college in Maryland, about the same time I entered Seton Hall. Then a mother of two teenagers, she consistently ranked at the top of her class. Many times when I struggled with a class, I thought about how tough it must have been for her to juggle school and family. Yet she consistently outperformed her younger peers, most of whom had the luxury of concentrating solely on school.

"You know what? I can do it, too," I said to myself.

The graduates sat in large groups, divided by schools.

Because we were seated in alphabetical order, I sat next to other guys whose names began with J, guys I had sat next to for four years during major exams and classes that grouped us that way. We talked and goofed off for most of the ceremony.

Finally, it was time to receive our degrees.

The master of ceremonies called the Robert Wood Johnson School of Medicine, and the graduates all stood and moved toward the stage. One by one their names were called.

Then, "Dr. Sampson Davis . . ."

As I watched Sam walk across the stage, I sat still and quiet. Pride swirled through my body. I was thinking, "Man, we really did this." I thought of all we had been through together, from boys comparing sneakers on the schoolyard in junior high to men walking across the stage to become doctors. We had leapt into the unknown together and locked hands and pulled one another up, over, and through the rough spots. I remembered how much I had hurt for him when he had failed the state board exam, how I'd driven to Camden one and a half hours each way nearly every weekend after that to be there for him. I tried to get him to play basketball and just have some fun to get his mind off the results of that test. It was all I could do to show him that I cared and that he wasn't alone.

This was the fourth time Sam and I had graduated together: junior high, high school, college, and now medical and dental school, and the third time for me and Rameck.

Just before graduation, Rameck had placed so much faith in me that he became one of my first patients. He needed some dental work done, and instead of going to an established professional, he visited the clinic at the dental school about five different times so that I could fill a few of his teeth. I even performed a periodontal surgery on him. The credits I earned working on my boy helped me to graduate.

Sam, Rameck, and I had become brothers, accepting one another for who we were. I think that this allowed us to see past whatever qualities irked us about one another. Our relationship extended to our families. During medical school, Rameck lived with my aunt in Maryland rent-free so he could do a rotation at Howard University.

I didn't really feel proud of myself until I saw Sam and Rameck walk across the platform. I thought of all I had learned from them: Sam, the workhorse, the most doggedly determined person I'd ever met, who held so much inside, and Rameck, the skeptic and activist, who was outraged by injustice and always believed there was something he could do to make things right.

I like to think I brought foresight to our trio. I've always been able to think clearly and see through to the end of a situation before getting entangled in it. That saved our behinds a million times.

When Rameck, Sam, and I each crossed the stage to get our diplomas, our families and friends roared. Each of us had an entourage of at least twenty people sitting in every corner of the amphitheater. Afterward, classmates jokingly asked if we had hired cheering squads.

After graduation, Rameck, Sam, and I decided not to go out together. We had planned our first real vacation together, and we were leaving for Cancún the next morning. It was our treat for all of the spring breaks and summer vacations we had missed because we'd been studying or working, and for all of the trips our families couldn't afford to take while we were kids growing up in Newark.

I did, however, go to visit my father, who had arrived in town two days before my graduation. I had been so busy that I hadn't had time to see him. A couple of my friends went with me to his hotel room. All of us had a few drinks together and caught up. I shared with him what was going on in my life, and he talked a bit about his, nothing really deep. This was the way things were between my father and me. I had long ago accepted that. Before I left, he told me he was proud of me. An hour had passed. It was time for me to get home.

Early the next morning, I drove around the corner to get a newspaper from one of the street salesmen. I knew the story on us was scheduled to appear, but I didn't know on what page. I stuck my hand out of the car window and motioned for the newspaper salesman. He turned to walk toward me, and I could see the front page atop the stack of papers in the plastic vest he was wearing. As he got closer, the photo of three boys drew more sharply into focus. They were grade-school pictures of Rameck, Sam, and me.

We were on the front page.

I was blown away. Most of the time when I saw young black men on the front page of a newspaper, they had either committed a big crime or they were dead. Not this day, though.

Our childhood photos were above a larger photo of us congratulating one another after graduation. The story under-neath told all of Newark about our pact. I had no idea then that the headline would be prophetic. It read simply:

START OF SOMETHING BIG.

# 18

# GOODBYE

## *Rameck*

MA ALWAYS TALKED about retiring and moving to South Carolina. Soon after I began medical school, she did just that.

After having worked as a mail clerk at the Newark post office for twenty-eight years, she bought a beautiful three-bedroom house that sat on a cul-de-sac in a secluded neighborhood in Columbia, the state capital. She liked the slow pace and beauty of the area. Ma initially planned to sell the family house in Plainfield, but she decided to keep it when the offers were lower than expected. She also wanted to have a place for her children to go if any of them ever needed a place to stay.

It seemed that Ma would finally get to relax and enjoy the rest of her life. She had worked hard for so long. But in 1997, the family noticed that she didn't look well when she returned home to visit her youngest daughter, Nicole, who had just had a baby. Ma's stomach was swollen as though she were pregnant, her skin had darkened, and the whites of her eyes had a yellowish tint. My aunts urged her to see a doctor.

About two months later, Ma called and told Nicole that her doctor had diagnosed her with cirrhosis of the liver. The family kept it from me. By the time I found out, Ma was so sick that my uncle Sheldon, a schoolteacher in New York, was heading to Columbia for the summer to help take care of her.

"Something's wrong with her liver," my aunt said when she called to tell me.

My family often hid bad news from me while I was away at school. They didn't want me to worry. When I first heard about Ma, I didn't get alarmed, because she had bounced back quickly before when a chest aneurysm forced her early retirement from the post office. It was the only other time I had ever seen her sick.

But this time, Ma kept getting sicker. When it was time for my uncle to return to New York to go back to work, the family realized that Ma couldn't stay in South Carolina alone. She needed to move back to Plainfield to be closer to the family.

At first, she resisted. But reality forced her to give in.

When Ma moved back home, she didn't look like herself. She had lost so much weight that she was skinny. Her skin was so dry and scaly that she scratched all the time. But even on her sickest day, I never saw her break down or cry.

"Don't worry about me," she always said.

But I did worry. Ma was slipping away, and I knew it. Nothing in life had prepared me to lose the woman who had been as close as a mother to me. I lived one and a half hours away, but I drove to Plainfield as often as I could to visit her.

In my last year of medical school, Ma's liver began to fail. For months, she was transferred from one hospital to the next for treatment. She landed at Mount Sinai in Manhattan. Once, the doctors had to intubate her. I rushed to her bedside. She couldn't speak, but I sat next to her, stroked her hand, and assured her that everything would be all right. I had seen many patients this way, but now it was personal. Seeing my grandmother so uncomfortable helped me to be more sensitive to the patients I encountered in medical school during my clinical rotations. I even chose gastroenterology as my specialty because I wanted to understand what was going on with my grandmother and someday keep other patients from suffering as much as she suffered.

Doctors were unsure what had caused the cirrhosis. The family turned to me with their questions. I felt helpless. I was a medical student, not a seasoned specialist, and I didn't have any answers. Her doctor seemed to be guessing about the cause of her illness. When I told him that Ma was not a heavy drinker, he said that even an occasional binge on alcohol could have caused the problem. I was offended by the suggestion.

Only two things were certain: Ma needed a new liver soon, and if she didn't get one, she would die.

The hospital placed her on its list of people waiting for liver transplants, but the doctor explained that because the wait could be as long as a year, she would probably not live to get a new liver. The doctor also presented us with a riskier alternative. The diseased part of Ma's liver could be replaced with a piece of a healthy liver from a living donor. I volunteered immediately to be tested as a possible match. I was scared, but I loved my grandmother. I figured I was young and healthy and could rebound quickly after the surgery.

I talked to George and Sam about my decision.

"Do what you got to do, dog," they told me. "We'll be there for you."

I was prepared to go forward with testing for the procedure, but my mother, aunts, and uncles talked me out of it. They said they needed me to be healthy to communicate with the doctors and didn't want to put me at risk. Most of the other family members who were willing to be tested had been ruled out as potential donors by the hospital's list of criteria.

So we prayed and waited for a donor to be found elsewhere.

Ma's illness proved to be a trying time for our family. When she could no longer take care of herself, the finger-pointing began about who wasn't doing enough to help. Ma had always been the one who solved problems and brought calm. Without her mediation, matters often dissolved into chaos. My aunts and uncles sometimes went without speaking until the next crisis brought them together.

Through it all, Ma never stopped encouraging me.

"I'm so proud of you," she would say. "You're doing so good."

My graduation was approaching, and I prayed that Ma would be able to make it. I wanted her to see me walk across the stage and become Dr. Rameck Hunt. I wanted her to witness the miracle that her faith in me had brought.

On graduation day, I kept looking into the stands for my family. They had helped me as much as they could have. When I had begun medical school and couldn't afford the expensive books, my mother's brothers and sisters had pooled money and sent it to me every month for several months. I've always been very grateful to them for that. From my seat near the front of the auditorium, the faces in the crowd looked blurred. But one time as I scanned the room, I noticed someone sitting in a wheelchair in the aisle. I couldn't make out the face, but I knew it was Ma. She had been determined to see this day. When the ceremony ended, my family wheeled her down to greet me. I threw my arms around her. She couldn't have given me a more special gift.

About three weeks later, the hospital called Ma with good news. A donor for her had been located. She happened to be home alone, but she needed to get to the hospital right away. A liver can function outside the body for only a limited time. Ma called her children. Nicole contacted her husband, Hosea, who worked in Plainfield and was just about to leave for the day. He drove to Ma's house and, escorted by Port Authority police, rushed her to Mount Sinai. Other family members met him there and waited in the family room while she underwent the surgery. Doctors had told Hosea that the operation was expected to take six hours. There was a high risk that Ma could die during the surgery. But when the team of doctors emerged from the operating room two hours early, my aunts and uncles took that as a good sign. They were right. The surgery was a success. When I heard the good news, I felt hopeful for the first time in months that she would get better.

Ma's recovery was going so well that the doctor released her from the hospital within a week. She began to feel stronger and look healthier. But that lasted just a few days. On

June 19, 1999, the day before the family was scheduled to gather at a cookout in West Orange to celebrate my graduation, Ma developed a fever and had to return to the hospital. We didn't think it was serious because she had experienced a similar episode a couple of days earlier, and the fever had gone away.

The weather for the cookout was perfect—sunny and hot. A large crowd of my family and friends, including Sam and George, spent the afternoon eating, drinking, dancing, and playing cards. I kept in touch with the doctor by phone.

That night, Sam and I were out on a double date when Ma's doctor called me on my cellular phone. Her blood pressure had dropped to dangerously low levels, and the infection had crept all over her body. I needed to get to the hospital right away.

On the way there, I prayed that Ma would be okay, but somehow I knew she wouldn't. When I arrived, family members were crying and hugging one another in the family room just outside the intensive care unit.

Ma was gone.

In my grief, I needed answers. I needed to know who was to blame. Had the doctors sent Ma home too soon? Was the liver they transplanted infected already? What had gone wrong?

I pushed for an autopsy, but my family wouldn't hear of it. That wouldn't bring her back, they said. Nor would it erase my pain. It was the hardest thing I have ever done, but I accepted their decision.

I let her go.

# 19

# HOME AGAIN

*Sam*

AFTER GRADUATION, I moved back to Newark, into the house of a friend from high school, Mary Ann Jackson. It was a perfect arrangement. The Jacksons live in a modest three-level house in a working-class neighborhood just three and a half miles from Beth Israel. Mary Ann lives in an apartment on the first floor, and I rented a bedroom on the top level, next to her cousin, Frankie White. As soon as I moved in, Mary Ann's mother, Carole Jackson, became my second mother and welcomed me into her extended family. She cooked big meals, which were wonderful after long shifts at the hospital. Frankie cooked on weekends. Alex, a neighbor and another of Ms. Jackson's adopted soldiers, stopped by in the evenings to eat and socialize. Ms. Jackson and Frankie took great pride in their cooking, and I was more than happy to clean up the leftovers.

Though we were back home, in some ways it felt as though everything had changed. None of us could have predicted the kind of reaction that the newspaper story about us would generate.

We became every mother's son. Strangers approached us with hugs. One woman walked up to me and burst into tears. We began to get letters from single women, and we got telephone calls at work from church groups and nonprofit organizations that wanted us to tell our story to other young people. Practically everyone saw us as a unit.

"You're one of those three doctors," people we encountered on the street would say.

We quickly amassed $3,000 in gifts from speaking engagements, but we didn't want to divide the money and just blow it. We figured we could put the money to good use by giving it away as a college scholarship to a needy student. But we decided we could do even more. We could create a nonprofit foundation that would finance ongoing scholarships, as well as programs that would expose children living in poor communities to professionals, colleges, and careers. We wanted to do for children in our neighborhoods what we knew would have helped us. We researched and established the Three Doctors Foundation, Incorporated.

The publicity from the newspaper story had another unexpected effect. Strangers who showed up in the emergency room at Beth Israel began telling the hospital staff that they were related to me. It became a big joke.

One time, though, it wasn't funny. Three months into my residency, I was about to begin my morning shift in the intensive-care unit when a nurse approached me. A woman in a room down the hall had come in the night before and was suffering from AIDS-related pneumonia. She claimed to be my sister. I froze. I knew this time it was true. The patient down the hall was my older sister, Fellease.

For a moment I didn't know what to do. I hadn't imagined my professional and personal lives meeting this way. Should I tell everyone that she was my sister and rush to her bedside? How would I be able to maintain a professional demeanor while watching my sister suffer? And what would my colleagues think if they saw me break down?

I pushed those thoughts to the back of my mind. I couldn't worry about that now. My big sister needed me.

It wouldn't be the last time that Fellease or someone else I knew showed up at the hospital during my shift. One time, I barely missed an old friend.

Just three days before I began a rotation in trauma at the University of Medicine and Dentistry of New Jersey, one of the older guys who had been involved in the robbery with me was rushed to the emergency room with gunshot wounds to his hip and abdomen. Another guy had been quicker to pull the trigger during an argument in the projects. The medical staff operated to remove the bullets. But he died the next day. He had just turned thirty.

When I heard what happened, I hurt for my old friend and his family. I suddenly saw myself. Instead of turning out to be a young doctor treating guys like him, I could easily have ended up a hustler, lying on the gurney with bullet holes about to snuff out my life.

Incidents like those helped me to grow and find the thing
that had eluded me through all four years of medical school—
my purpose and place as a physician.

More times than not, the patients I treated were poor.
Sometimes they were drug dealers, addicts, prostitutes, or
drunks. I couldn't look down on them. I had brothers and sisters who suffered from mental illness and addiction. I had
been a thug myself. I realized that the only thing that separated my patients from me was opportunity, and the support
of family and friends. No matter what state they were in when
they came to me for treatment, I never judged them.

"Hey, I know you," I would say with a big smile when a
familiar face showed up in the emergency room. "You know
I'm gonna take care of you."

I saw relief in their eyes and knew why I needed to be a
doctor.

I discovered that peace of mind follows purpose. All of
the misery and doubt that I had felt over the past four years
disappeared.

In my evaluations, the head doctors said things like, "I've
never seen a guy so happy to be at work," "I've never seen a
guy interact as well with the ancillary staff as he does with the
head staff," "I've never seen another guy who can bring a smile
to a patient's face no matter what kind of day he is having."

For the first time in years, I was truly happy. I had overcome so much, and there were regular reminders of that.

In my second year of residency, I received a subpoena to
testify at a rape trial. I had treated the alleged victim in the
emergency room and had to testify to her physical condition.

As I walked up the courthouse steps that day, it dawned on me that this was the same building where I had met regularly with my probation officer a decade earlier.

This time, I was returning as a doctor. During the hearing, I would be deemed an expert witness.

Now that I was back home, I got to spend more time with family and old friends from the neighborhood, particularly my boy Will.

William Cortez was one of the first real friends I ever had. He lived across the street from me with his mother and younger brother in Building 6 of the Dayton Street Projects. We met playing sponge ball in the neighborhood, and before long the two of us and Noody and another friend, Jermaine, were hanging together all the time.

Like mine, Will's family struggled. On many days he had to eat at his grandmother's house because there was no food at home. And like me, he was seduced for a short time by the thrills of the street. The day I got involved in the armed robbery, we had stopped by Will's house to pick him up. But he had a new girlfriend, and he told her to tell us he wasn't there.

When I left for college, Will had dropped out of high school and was working in the housekeeping department at a nearby hospital. His girlfriend was pregnant. He was so happy for me when I told him I was going to college.

"At least somebody's gonna do it," he told me.

That's what I liked about Will. He was a positive brother who always encouraged me, even during the rough times in medical school when I called him and talked about dropping out.

"Naw, man, there ain't nothing back here for you," he would tell me. "I'm proud of you. You got brothers like me looking up to you."

We were cooling out in my room one day before I left for college when he asked me to be his daughter's godfather. My mouth dropped open. I had this expression on my face, like, "Me?" He was my boy, and the gesture meant so much.

I was in medical school in January of 1995 when Will called and told me he had been shot. He had stopped at a stop sign in his gray-and-white Oldsmobile Achiever when a car full of guys pulled up next to him and started staring him down. Suddenly, one of the passengers jumped out and started shooting into Will's car. The guy fired at least ten rounds with a .45, striking Will in the chin near his neck and his front-seat passenger in the face and arm. Broken glass from the shattered car window grazed the backseat passenger on the ear. Two of Will's friends, following behind him in another car, were also shot.

Unbeknownst to Will, the guy in his backseat, an acquaintance he was giving a ride home, had gotten into a beef with the shooter at a bar earlier. Will survived the injuries, but for a long time, the shooting made him leery of meeting new people. Even so, when I introduced Will to George and Rameck, the three of them instantly hit it off. Will wasn't the least bit threatened by or jealous of my relationship with the two of them. If anything, he co-signed the friendship pact and became a part of it, once even vacationing with the three of us.

George, Rameck, and I each kept up ties with some of the more positive brothers from our old neighborhoods, and the other two of us would embrace him as part of our group. Will was at our graduation, he was there many times when the three of us gave speeches in the community or received awards, and he began hanging out with us when the three of us returned to Newark as doctors.

One of the most gratifying things to happen when I returned to Newark was my relationship with my oldest brother, Kenny. Kenny, who had been paralyzed on his right side, was living in a residential home for the disabled in a suburb called Cedar Grove. As a kid, I had always admired him, but he was often so mean to me that I wondered whether he loved me. Before his injury, our relationship had been strained. But I began to visit him regularly, and I could feel us getting closer. Every time I went to see him, he had a hundred people—doctors, nurses, other staff, and patients—who he wanted me to meet.

During one of my visits, just before Christmas in 2000, he casually handed me a plastic bag.

"This is your Christmas present," he said.

I was surprised. I couldn't remember the last time Kenny had given me a Christmas present. I opened the bag. Inside was a big, green leather photo album. A few days later, when I had a little downtime at home, I pulled out my new photo album to start filling it with pictures. On the cover was something I hadn't noticed: DR. SAMPSON MARSHALL DAVIS, 1999, in gold press-on letters.

He had obviously worked on it during his crafts workshop. I flipped the album open to the first page to start arranging my pictures, but there was another surprise. It read:

*Marshall, I admire you, and I'm proud of all your accomplishments. The following pages will prove it to you. Love, your brother, Kenny.*

He had saved and collected old photos—every graduation program and newspaper article that mentioned my name, even my old report cards and diploma from grade school.

I'm not one to cry easily. But the tears came faster than I could swallow. It was the best gift I've ever received.

Every successful career has defining moments, those times when you know deep down that you're doing what you were meant to do and you're good at it. For me, those moments have been as simple as seeing the gratitude in a patient's eyes or as grand as watching a patient you've fought to save gradually come back to life. Sometimes, though, it is even in the agony of falling short after giving everything you've got.

*April 19, 2001, about 9:15 P.M.*

I was stitching a patient's mouth when I suddenly heard chaos—doors slamming and people shouting and rushing down the hall. I finished and stepped out of the door.

"Someone's been shot," I heard in the commotion.

I ran outside and saw a young man, about my age, holding his torso, bent over, stumbling around. Blood covered his shirt and pants. I took his hand and helped the staff put him on a stretcher. We quickly wheeled him into the emergency room. I counted six gunshot wounds.

I observed his chest and checked his airway to make sure he was breathing normally and there were no airway obstructions. He was alert enough to tell me that he had been standing on the corner when some guys walked up and shot him.

"How old are you, man?" I asked, trying to keep him calm as I worked to save his life.

"Thirty-three," he said softly.

I ran an intravenous line into his blood vessels to pump fluids into him as quickly as possible. He was losing too much blood.

He looked up at me.

"Doc, I'm gonna die," he said. "There's nothing you can do."

I put a tube down his throat to open his airway, cut a small incision in his chest, and inserted a separate tube to expand his lungs, which had collapsed.

"Stay with me, man. I'm here," I said. "I'm with you."

One thing I had learned in my short career was that when a patient tells you he is going to die, you'd better listen.

My patient closed his eyes, and within minutes the rhythmic thump of the monitor became a shrill, steady beep. A flat line appeared on the screen.

His heart had stopped. We were losing him.

"Stay with me, man. Stay with me," I shouted.

I immediately began CPR. He didn't respond.

Time was running out.

A surgeon who had responded to my page and was standing at the patient's bedside took over and performed a thoracotomy, a last-minute lifesaving procedure in which a patient's chest is opened to evaluate the heart and major vessels and look for holes in those structures. Sure enough, my colleague discovered a hole in a ventricle of the heart.

By then, our patient was dead.

"I'm sorry," I said to his wife and mother at the man's bedside a short while later. "We did everything we could to save him."

"You should have done more!" the mother yelled at me. She was hurting. I knew it. I just wish she could have known how much I was hurting, too. I had worked nearly two hours to save her son's life. And I had done everything humanly possible to bring him back. I had already asked myself if I could have done more. Still, I would go home and read more, study more, try to improve, and pray that just maybe next time I could help more.

That, to me, is what being a doctor is all about.

As I left the room, the director of the residency program pulled me aside in the hall. I was in no mood for questions. What did he want?

"I just want to congratulate you," he said.

I gave him the strangest look. I had just lost a patient, and my boss was congratulating me?

"You scored very well on the in-service exam, one of the best in the class," he said.

He was referring to the exam that residents at hospitals across the country take each year to test their proficiency in their specialties. It is the profession's way of gauging how a resident is doing in the field. My score was above average for the nation.

I had risen to the top of the class.

Sometime later, Rameck, George, and I got together to celebrate my performance on the test, George's birthday, and all the blessings we'd received to that point. We met at a night-club and ordered drinks.

When the drinks arrived, we raised our glasses high. No need for a bunch of corny words. We knew what we had been through.

"To friends," we said one at a time, clinking our glasses together in a triumphant toast.

# EPILOGUE

IT REALLY MAKES us feel good when we finish a speech at a school, church, or community center and kids come up to us in their cliques and say they're going to form their own pact. When the three of us promised in high school to see one another through to becoming doctors, we had no idea how we'd make it. We honestly didn't even give it much thought. But we've realized since then that each of us was successful individually in large part because of our pact.

The pact filled us with motivation and purpose, giving us a reason to keep pushing when it would have been easier just to give up. It provided us with a firm base of support, and it strengthened us to face the challenges that came our way. So we've come up with a few pieces of advice to help others unite with friends to reach short- or long-term goals. We believe these steps can be useful to the group, no matter what the goal is:

- Join trustworthy friends who have the same goal. George was the one who put our pact together. Though two of us—Rameck and Sam—initially had different ideas about what we wanted to do after high school, we eventually came around to George's way of thinking about going to Seton Hall.

- Find strength in your differences. Friends don't have to be alike to be part of a pact. The three of us all have distinct personalities that we bring to the mix, and that just makes our bond all the more interesting and stronger. We draw from one another's strengths. For example, when George began dental school alone, he relied on study tactics that he'd learned from Sam, the workhorse, to become more disciplined. It was Rameck who pushed us to form the mentoring group Ujima in college. And George was the one who pulled Rameck back when he was set on becoming a rapper. To be able to keep our promise to one another, we first had to want the same thing. The few times when our promise threatened to break apart was when one of us began to want something different from what the other two wanted. We also had to trust one another completely. We had to believe that we had one another's back, or crazy suspicions of one another's motives might have driven us apart.

- Believe in yourself and your friends. After we graduated

from high school, Rameck's younger sister, Daaimah, ended up with the same biology teacher that he'd had— the one he didn't like. When Daaimah told the teacher that she was Rameck's sister, the teacher asked whether he had become a bum. "No," Daaimah said proudly. "He's a doctor." That teacher may not have believed that Rameck was ever going to do anything positive with his life, but all three of us knew he was smart and would find a way to make a positive difference in the world. All three of us had—and still have—that kind of faith in one another. It just doesn't make much sense to hook up with somebody you can't believe in.

- Compete in a healthy way. This is a biggie, because healthy competition pushed each of us to be at the top of our game all the time. Each of us wanted to perform as well as the other two. But understand that healthy competition is just that—healthy, which means there is no room for jealousy. Jealousy would have brought too much negative energy to our group; it would have made us question the trust that is so integral to our friendship and to the very nature of a pact. If any of us ever felt even a bit envious of the others, it never surfaced in a way that was obvious to us. We celebrated one another's successes, and each one of us felt the same hurt when one of our boys failed at something. We learned from one another and leaned on one another's strengths. George taught us that looking ahead not only helps you plan for the future but also helps you avoid the obvious pitfalls. Sam showed us how to work harder than we ever had before and how to keep pushing in any situation. And from Rameck, we learned that tough questions, even skepticism, always have a place.

- Communicate openly, honestly, and often. This kept us sane. We hung out together and talked every day about what we were going through. We compared notes and gave one another advice and suggestions. Rameck and Sam were roommates for all eight years, and to be successful at it, they learned to talk out their differences better than many married couples. There were times, though, when we kept things from one another; times when sharing our feelings was difficult. We blame that on just being guys. In our case, the stereotype—guys don't share their feelings with one another—was definitely true. If we have any regrets, that's probably chief among them. Our inability to communicate when Sam felt like he was dying inside forced him to look outside the group for support. There was nothing wrong with that, except we risked isolating him and leaving him feeling resentful. Fortunately for us, things didn't turn out that way.

- Lean on your friends and allow them to lean on you. This is just an extension of the friendship bond. But it becomes particularly important when you're working together to reach a goal, because the pact essentially ties your fates together. One of the main benefits of forming a pact with friends is that you have an automatic network of support. You shouldn't have to seek elsewhere to find it.

The three of us didn't truly realize how much we had accomplished together until we started working on this book. Of course we understood the magnitude of our achievements—we can hardly believe them ourselves. But working together on this project, going over our years together, we feel great pride. And we also feel awe—at the power of friendship, a power greater than any one of us could have individually. After writing this book, we see more clearly than ever that we needed one another to achieve our dreams. Even as we write, we are just weeks away from completing our residencies. Sam will be starting as an Emergency Room Attending Physician, a head doctor, at Beth Israel Hospital in Newark. George will be an administrator and Assistant Professor at the University of Medicine and Dentistry of New Jersey in Newark, and he is working on his Master's in public health. Rameck will be starting as an Assistant Professor and director of the outpatient clinic at St. Peter's University Hospital in New Brunswick, just a few miles away.

Our pact has extended beyond anything we could ever have imagined in high school. Through our nonprofit organization, the Three Doctors Foundation, we hope to inspire and create opportunities for inner-city communities by providing education, mentoring, and health awareness. The foundation is a vehicle through which we do our community work. We do public speaking engagements together. We go to schools, colleges, churches, and even corporations to share our story.

We've come a long way from the streets of Newark in some ways, but not far at all in others. Our hearts are still with the families and friends who didn't have the opportunities, the

friendships, or maybe even the crazy dreams that were somehow given to us—those who are still struggling every day just
to survive.

They are the reason we wrote this book.

—*Dr. Sampson Davis, Dr. George Jenkins,*
*and Dr. Rameck Hunt*

# ACKNOWLEDGMENTS

THE STORY OF our lives and friendship is in many ways also the story of our families and friends. We'd like to thank them for the courage they displayed throughout this project and the trust they placed in us as we shared the good and the bad. Much of this book is about the positive influences that people along the way had on us, yet there were times when some members of our families and friends were victims of circumstances that didn't allow them to be there for us, and some even caused us pain—either knowingly or unknowingly. It is possible that if we hadn't faced those difficulties, we wouldn't have had the conviction and motivation to make it to where we are today, or the empathy for others that our experiences afforded us. We are truly grateful and feel tremendously blessed by the love and generosity that our families have demonstrated toward us. Our individual thanks are listed below. But first, all three of us collectively would like to thank the great many individuals and institutions that helped to transform all three of our lives. Among them are: our classmates, and the teachers, advisers, and other staff who supported us at University High School, Seton Hall University, the Robert Wood Johnson Medical School, and the University of Medicine and Dentistry of New Jersey in Newark. We are forever indebted to Carla Dickson, who was surely sent by God to guide us through. We owe much of our success to the Pre-Medical/Pre-Dental Plus Program and Access Med, two affirmative-action programs that simply gave us a chance. If we had lived in other states where such programs have come under attack, we probably would not have been afforded the opportunities that helped to make us who we are.

We are grateful to our agent, Joann Davis, whose hard work and guidance set this book in motion, and to our editor at Riverhead, Cindy Spiegel, whose creative ideas made this a better book.

To Dr. Noble and Mrs. Mann, thanks for realizing before anyone else—even us—that we had a story to tell. Only God could have predicted this book. We never knew our story would reach so far and touch so many. To all who helped us convey our message of hope, we say thanks, particularly:

To Caryl Lucas, who wrote the first *Star-Ledger* article that turned into many more; Kaylyn Dines, who stayed behind us and made things happen; Karriem and Veronica Salaam, Elayne Fluker, and Terrie Williams, for finding us worthy of national recognition; Windy Smith, James Keyes, and Greg Collins, for all your work with the Three Doctors Foundation; Bernard McArthur and Sean "P. Diddy" Combs, for being the first people to donate to the foundation; Kim Holiday, for all your work with the Web site development; Congressman Payne, for opening your doors; Bobbi, for stepping up and helping us whenever we needed your support; Jo-Marie, for being there in the beginning; Susan Taylor, Ed Lewis, and Clarence Smith, for introducing us to the world; and finally, to Lisa Frazier Page, for the many exhausting hours put into this project, your relentless effort, and your understanding in all matters. When you and your husband, Kevin, were blessed with two children during the course of this project, we felt only joy for the two of you and realized that Kevin, Kevin Jr., and Danielle would only strengthen you and help to make this endeavor a success. You were truly God-sent.

*From George Jenkins:*

This effort is dedicated to the people and things that make me who I am, and why:

1. My people, for always believing in me and never doing anything but support and nurture my aspirations.

2. My city, specifically the Central Ward. Right now, as I sit to write this acknowledgment, about fifteen teenagers dressed in red are gathered on the corner across the street around a '92-ish white Honda Accord that's doing doughnuts in the street to all of the kids' delight. And I'm thinking to myself, like an old, experienced man (There the screeches go again, as I write at 10:05 P.M. on January 5, 2002, no lie):

Where are their parents? Where are the cops? I'm thinking this, despite the fact that I didn't call the cops, right or wrong. Where I live, that's street survival code: Volume 1, Rule #1. But I'm also wondering: Where are our young leaders to show the kids something different from what they see around here? And the first thing that comes to my mind is that Sam, Rameck, and I have a lot of work to do, real soon. I think, too, for a moment, "Damn, I got to move." But where can I go where they want me more than here, despite its challenges? Living here fills me with so much purpose and determination for change that I can't even begin to help you understand if you don't already. I really can see the change when I daydream, so I have to believe it can be done. Nothing's sweet on this route, but I play the hand I was dealt with my head up high because I know that every day I'm becoming more and more equipped academically to spin that old globe in Ms. Johnson's class and pick a spot. I'll bet it would land on brick city every time. Thank you, Ms. Johnson, for the jewels you placed in my mind.

3. My circle, for all you do: Garland, Sam, Rameck, Shahid, Na-im, Tone Webb, Roz, Faye, Orlando, Ant Brown and Al Brown.

4. My classmates, UHS Class of '91 and NJDS Class of '99, especially Rhoda Pruitt, Alicia Grey, Cathleen Woods, and Denise Davis, for all the lessons we learned together.

5. My other father, Shahid Jackson, Sr., for being there. You always believed in me. I believe in you, too, as you make one of your dreams come true by launching your own private security firm, Forje's.

6. My block, for keeping it real: Reggie and Kenny, Lace, Tiffy, Steffy and Kenyor, Mandy, Bruce and Gett, Hak and Fuquan, Smiley, Marv, Samad, Brian Jackson, Usef, Sneaky Pete, Shoronda and Malika, Sockie and Vonetta, Lebrashaun and family, Rahman and Abdul, Denaaman, Sherri and the Washingtons, the Seaburns, Farad (Hold your head up. I'm riding with you) and the Greens, Anwar, Toy and little Puff (I see you winning computers and things for an essay on me at school. Keep it up), Rasheed Jackson, Brian, the counselor at the Central Ward Boys' Club (Thanks for being something different from what was all around me at the time), Chuck and Wop (Thanks for starting elementary school with me and, despite whatever changes you had to face, always encour-

aging me to keep it moving). When your community encourages you, rather than tears you down, great things can come from nothing at all. RIP—Anton, Duane, Brian McKoy, Wayne Smiley, and Ms. Willie Mae.

7. My mom, for all you did—and still do—for me. Because you had the drive to get your son's crooked teeth fixed for his future, you inadvertently provided one of the biggest inspirations for his future. You have always tirelessly given so much of yourself to make sure I was on point or could concentrate on school as much as possible, and you are the root of my inspiration, whether you realize it or not. Just know that I love you for all your dedication and that I will always have your back the way you had mine, Ma Dukes. I deeply appreciate you with all my heart even when I am not showing it, please believe it.

8. A certain NBA star, Allen Iverson, for his determination to be who he is and his refusal to allow his profession to force him to be someone else and dissociate from the place and the people who made him who he is. I found that very inspiring at times in my situation. It was cool to see him win the NBA's MVP award after all the bad press he received for his conviction.

9. Finally, a dusty book I found about four years ago—*A Pictorial History of the Negro in America,* by Langston Hughes and Milton Meltzer—for its impact on my life. I opened it because, ever since Ms. Johnson's class, I'll thumb through encyclopedias or similar books to read about places and things of the world. Published in 1956, the book by Hughes and Meltzer chronicles my people's history and, as the foreword says, "the feel and the mood of each passing phase of the past 350 years," ending in 1954, when my mom was six. I would come to revere it like an archaeological discovery, and it would teach me about people like John Russworm, the first person of color to graduate from an American college, Bowdoin College in Maine in 1826. As I read I was thinking, like, "If he did it then, what is my problem with the self-pity?" An article by Eric Pooley that I once read said something like, "There is a bright magic at work when one aspiring leader reaches into the past and finds another waiting to guide him." That's sort of how it felt, but more like a jolting kick, especially when, as I was closing the book, I noticed on the front cover two signatures that appeared to be the authors'. At the time, I hadn't heard of Mr. Meltzer, but I stroked the ink of Langston

Hughes's signature over and over, hardly able to believe it was authentic. I later mentioned the signatures to Ernestine Watson, the director of the special vendors program at the UMDNJ, who did some research and helped convince me that the signatures are in fact authentic. In every old document she found containing Langston Hughes's signature, that beautiful swooshing "L" flowed as smooth as Nike's logo, and that wonderful cross of the "t" in his first name made it to the first line of the "H" in his last. After four years I still thumb through the book when I'm relaxing, and I learn something fresh every time. Hughes's signature actually inspired me to start writing my own feelings down on paper, which later turned into poems, which at times serve as my personal therapy. If it weren't for that book and those signatures, I would be totally devoid of the knowledge of relevant individuals who fought for my path to simply exist, even with all the obstacles. I would never have learned what it feels like to write a poem, read it back, and say, "Now, finally, somebody knows what I'm talking about," and feel instantly better. Funny thing, I e-mailed my first couple of poems to Sam and Rameck for feedback, and they said, "Oh, yeah, dog, they're cool, word up, real deep." I was laughing so hard at how uncomfortable they seemed. To my boys, Sam and Rameck: I know y'all didn't really get them, but, as always, the encouragement I was looking for was there in a hilarious kind of way that only I would see. Maybe I'll let you guys read some more one day, when you knuckleheads open your fat heads up a little. No beef, just laughter, and besides, that's just simply how we get down.

*From Sampson Davis:*

To my mother: after God comes you. Thank you for not giving up and running out on us. You are by far the strongest person I have ever known. I love you with all that I have. Realize that faith can overcome all. You taught me to put God first and the rest will follow. To my father, thank you for being there for me. You taught me how to be a man. Your dedication and dignity taught me how to stand tall and face my responsibilities in good and bad times. To my brothers and sisters, I am so proud of the bond we have developed. You are all a part of me, and we will always remain a tight unit. Kenny, Rose, Fell, Andre, and Carlton, I shared our lives in an attempt to help others. There are so many people in life who have similar endeavors and need to know there are other people out there living the same life. We all know that as long as we live there are going to be ups and downs. I call it your own personal roller coaster. All of you are winners. Success is not based on financial gain or easy winnings. It is based on how well you take advantage of timing and opportunity and get back up once you have fallen. To all of my mentors—Carla, Dr. Hsu, Reggie, Dr. Essien, Mom, Pop, countless teachers and doctors—you are the educators. Sometimes we ask what is the purpose of our daily lives. Here is your answer: a success story that can't be made up. I have found that it is better to give, even when you don't have much to give. When I speak to kids about their future and to adults about their health, there is nothing more rewarding than that warm look of gratitude when you know you have made a difference. And believe me, you all have touched my life. Without you, there would be no me. I often say that if I had one big room, I would be able to fill it with those who helped me make it to where I am today. I am forever grateful and will never forget where I came from. We all know that to go where you are going you must know where you came from. To the city of Newark—we did it. My work is for the kids who wish to achieve, for the adults who still believe. It can be done. There have been people in my life who told me that I couldn't do this. To them, I give thanks—because you are the ones who made me dig deeper than I even imagined and reach heights that I once thought were unattainable. I had to learn how to use negative environments as inspiration. I was constantly telling myself, "I may not know what it is I want to do, but I know for sure I don't want to do that. After all, how many retired drug dealers do you see drawing a pension?"

To my sister Fellease, whom I lost to AIDS during the writing of this book, I miss you so much—your laugh, your stories, your smile. I never will forget the times we had together. Man, life seemed so simple then. Although we were poor, we never focused too much on it because we always had love. My purpose of sharing your struggles is to open the doors of communication with others who may be struggling the same way. I never knew how to deal with a disease like AIDS in such a personal way until it happened at home. I thought we would live forever, growing old, sharing our stories. But our destinies were written differently. You taught me how to live life for the moment, how to make the most out of every situation. I never saw a stronger fighter. Sis, you fought it to the end. You never lost faith, you never gave up, and you never lost that smile. You never knew that during my darkest moment I would look at your struggle and say to myself, "Damn, if she can fight, so can I." You helped propel me when my tank was on empty. You also helped me to realize that it was okay to let go, it was okay to laugh, and it was okay to smile in times of mourning. That is how you lived life, and, after all, you wouldn't have wanted it any other way. I've never in my life seen someone who made more out of a bad situation than you. Thank you for believing in me. You were always my bullhorn, making sure everyone knew I was your brother, The Doctor. My regret is simple: that I couldn't do more. I miss you, Sis, and will see you on the other side. Love ya.

To Carla, my earth angel—how many times have you placed the three of us before yourself? You are priceless.

To Will—it always amazed me that we don't have to see each other for six months and still pick up like we left it.

To Dax, my conscious bro'—you never passed judgment and always lent an ear.

To Camille—you're the sis my mother didn't have and my backbone.

To Sabu—coming back to the city enhanced our relationship. See you at the lounge.

To the Jacksons—thank you for opening your home to me. It's funny how three months became three years.

To D—hold it down, big dawg, it's almost over.

To Noody—we still got it, big dawg. The series is tied 132–132.

For those whose names I didn't mention, know that you, too, are a part of my success, and I thank you.

I must single out my boys, Gee and Rah. Man, we have did it all. We couldn't have planned this outcome, even if we tried. It is amazing what can happen if you just take a chance, a step out on faith. Our road traveled was a blind venture. Many times we tripped over our own shoelaces. But we never stop believing in one another. We laughed, we cried, we hugged, we danced, we argued, and we smiled. Most of all, we believed. Thank you for the ride. There is nothing the three of us can't accomplish. It is now, as always, our responsibility to continue to help all others.

*From Rameck Hunt:*

First and foremost, I'd like to thank God. Truly God deserves all the credit and praise because without Him, there would be no us. God took three young boys and made them into men. Through us He is showing the world what miracles are made of and is spreading a message—a message of perseverance, true friendship, love, dedication, and trust. He teaches us the lesson of caring and giving back, each one teach one. Only God could produce the miracle that we are, and to Him I am forever thankful.

I am so thankful that I have friends and family to share my life and my love. I feel really loved, and I thank you all and love you so much, especially:

My mother, for instilling values in me early on. Without them I don't know if I would have made it. Even though we had our share of problems through the years, what you taught me will last a lifetime. I love you so much, Mom.

My father, for listening to me when I needed you. Just watching you and listening to you reminds me that I came from your seed. We are so much alike, and I am proud and thankful that I inherited such wonderful genes. Love you, Dad. Thank you for all the lessons you taught me.

My late grandmother, Ellen Bradley, a tear is shed even as I write this. I love you and I know you are my angel, watching over me.

My sisters, Daaimah, Mecca, and Quamara. I love all of you and I would do anything in this world for you. Thank you for loving me. You may not know it, but just checking up on me from time to time meant so much to me.

My aunts and uncles, Rasheed, Sheldon, Gloria, Nicole, Victoria, Venus, Rahman, Teresa, Kenny, and the late Anthony and Jackie, I love you all. Thanks for being there for me.

My cousins, thanks for keeping me humble. I'm still Mr. Potato Head.

My friends. I learned a lot from all of you, bad and good, lessons that I will take with me always, lessons that made me who I am. I'm so glad to see that so many of you, like me, have changed your lives and are doing the right things.

The love of my life, continue to stand by me and hold me down like you do.

And Nana. You showed me the importance of family (and Sunday dinner).

The brothers I never had: Sam and George. We have been through a lot together and will go through so much more. But I want both of you to know how much I appreciate your friendship. "I am my brother's keeper," as I'm sure you are mine.

*From Lisa Frazier Page:*

I give all honor, glory, and praise to the Lord of my life, Jesus Christ, who makes what seems impossible possible. I would not have been able to participate in this project without the unwavering love and dedication of my husband, Kevin, who answered my kazillion computer questions, kept me calm, and took care of our home so I could focus on this book. In the year I spent working on the book, I became a mother twice—to Danielle, our beautiful baby girl, brought home for adoption at nearly six months old, and Kevin Jr., our baby boy and symbol of hope, born six months later on September 12, 2001, the day after the World Trade Center and Pentagon tragedies. I thank my two miracle babies and my awesome teenage daughter, Enjoli, for the joy and wonder that keep me sane. I'm blessed with a large network of family and friends who supported me in large and small ways. To each of you, especially my parents, Clinton and Nettie Frazier, and the parents I inherited, Richard and Miriam Page, I am eternally grateful. Thanks to my supportive colleagues, friends, and editors at *The Washington Post* and my other friends in the business, particularly Wil Haygood, who was there all the way to read as much, as often, and as quickly as I needed and who offered invaluable critique, advice, and encouragement. Thanks to Joann Davis, for all you did to make this book a success, and to Cindy Spiegel, for your brilliant editing and desire to get this right. And to three incredible guys—Drs. Sampson Davis, Rameck Hunt, and George Jenkins—thanks for your faith in me. If you ever worried whether my two new babies would overwhelm your baby, this book, you never showed it. Thanks for your inspiration. And most of all, thanks for our new friendship.

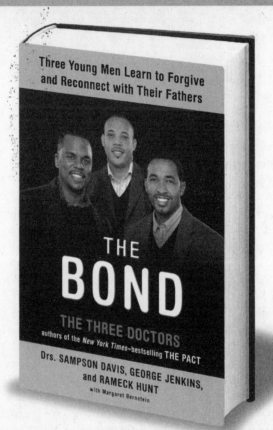